GRUNDY'S TAX HAVENS

AUSTRALIA
The Law Book Company Ltd.
Sydney : Melbourne : Brisbane

INDIA
N. M. Tripathi Private Ltd.
Bombay

ISRAEL
Steimatzky's Agency Ltd.
Jerusalem : Tel Aviv : Haifa

MALASIA : SINGAPORE : BRUNEI
Malayan Law Journal (Pte.) Ltd.
Singapore

NEW ZEALAND
Sweet & Maxwell (N.Z.) Ltd.
Wellington

PAKISTAN
Pakistan Law House
Karachi

U.S.A. and CANADA
Matthew Bender & Co. Inc.
New York

GRUNDY'S
TAX HAVENS

A WORLD SURVEY

Edited by
MILTON GRUNDY, M.A. (CANTAB.)
of the Inner Temple and Gray's Inn, Barrister-at-Law

LONDON
SWEET & MAXWELL

NEW YORK
MATTHEW BENDER
& CO. INC.

1972

First Edition (Etablissement Général des Instituts Financiers) 1969
Second Edition (Sweet & Maxwell: Matthew Bender & Co. Inc.) 1972

*Published in Great Britain by
Sweet & Maxwell Ltd. of
11 New Fetter Lane, London*

*Published in the U.S.A. by
Matthew Bender & Co. Inc. of
235 East 45th Street,
New York, N.Y. 10017*

*Printed in Great Britain by
Ebenezer Baylis & Son Ltd.
The Trinity Press
Worcester, and London*

SBN 421 17260 6

Library of Congress Catalog Card No. 72-78-531

PREFACE

THIS volume contains the basic information about the principal tax havens, stated as at 1st January, 1972. The territories covered are those in the first edition, with the addition of the New Hebrides and Norfolk Island.

As I said in the preface to the first edition, in editing a work of this kind, the first problem is one of definition: what is a tax haven? In selecting the territories which merit inclusion in this work, I have had regard to a number of factors—communications, political stability, freedom of currency movement, availability of professional and financial services—as well as the nature and level of direct taxation, and I have asked the contributors to mention any relevant aspects of these in their several contributions; I have also taken it as axiomatic that the fiscal advantages offered by the territory concerned should be of a general nature and not merely of limited application to too narrow a range of circumstances. On these grounds I have excluded a number of territories[1] which I regard as failing to meet one or more of these requirements or which, while retaining in the public mind the aura of fiscal paradise, no longer offer any substantial facilities for international transactions. There are of course some borderline cases, and I would not pretend that my researches have any claim to completeness; but I hope my omissions do not give rise to any offence.

The nature of this work is such that it can make no more than a passing reference to the vast network of double taxation conventions; and it is of course not at all the place to attempt any treatment of what can so often be the most difficult problems associated with any tax haven transaction, namely those arising from the laws and practices which domestically circumscribe the activities and determine the tax liabilities of the parties.

I have asked the contributors to indicate the nature of the entities which are known to their local law and where relevant to mention the kind of use which can be made of them by persons whose residence or main seat of business is outside that territory. As to who precisely uses

[1] Andorra, Antigua, Bahrein, Barbados, Campione, Eire, Greece, Haiti, Jamaica, Lebanon, Malta, Monaco, Netherlands, Nauru, St. Vincent, Sark, Turks and Caicos Islands, Uruguay.

tax havens, or—perhaps more importantly—to what extent, it seems impossible even to make a guess: as far as individual users are concerned at any rate (as opposed to the public and international corporations) there is some evidence to suggest that they are searching for privacy as much as for financial or fiscal benefit.[2] So far as I am able to discover there is in this area a complete absence of anything one could seriously call statistical material. This has not prevented a good deal of criticism being levelled at the tax havens—on the grounds that they have permitted themselves to be used for manipulation of the world's currency markets, or for salting away the proceeds of criminal activities, or to enable a wealthy person to conceal his income and fortune from the community in which he is content to live. I have spoken to most of the contributors on this subject, and they are undoubtedly sensitive to criticism of this kind, particularly since no serious evidence appears to have been adduced to support the view that such activities are more prevalent in their territories than in New York, Frankfurt or Buenos Aires.[3] The general view which I have gathered is that the tax havens must cause some loss to the fiscal authorities throughout the world; but there must also be some truth in the proposition that a good deal of business is done via tax havens which, if the parties were contemplating a net-after-tax return, would not get done at all.

Perhaps the most notable change which has affected tax havens in the three years since the first edition of this book is in the extent to which the subject has become discussable. This may be attributable to the wave of press and public discussion which occurred during the rise and fall of the Off-shore Mutual Fund, or it may simply be part of the general tendency for taboo subjects to become discussable; at all events, the tax havens are now a recognized part of the world's financial geography and one hears less of "international centres" and suchlike euphemisms. This is a trend to be welcomed, for in the end, I suppose, the world gets the tax havens it wants: at a practical level it seems plain that there is a demand for a freedom of manœuvre—in deprecia-

[2] See P. Ferris: *Men and Money* (Hutchinson, 1968), Chapter 7. The notorious "numbered account" can carry a derisory interest rate and dividends paid to a tax haven almost invariably suffer a higher rate of withholding tax.

[3] Vernay: *Les Paradis Fiscaux* (Editions du Seuil, 1968) notes that the principal tax havens—as can be seen from the contents of this book—are for the most part under the British flag or under powerful U.S. influence, and advances the intriguing theory that they are part of the mechanism whereby La Wall Street and La City impose upon the world "la hégémonie anglo-saxonne".

tion, profit accumulation and investment-switching, in privacy, in provision for inheritance, and in numerous other respects, and that the tax havens are responding to this demand in a very active way.[4]

It may well be that a volume of this kind enables anyone with a tolerably good memory to become an International Tax Expert; its aim, nevertheless, is both more serious and more modest, and that is to give the reader a general idea of what can and cannot be achieved in the various tax havens, so as to enable him to decide, in the context of a particular problem, no more than that one or another territory appears to fit the bill. At this point, I intend that the inquirer should address himself to someone experienced in that territory. The contributors to this book were selected because of their expertise in this field and they would each be happy to deal with readers' inquiries regarding their respective territories.

Once again I should like to express my thanks to all the organizations which have provided the contributions to this book and in particular to their various executives, senior staff, lawyers and accountants who have kindly set aside time for meetings with me, and have had to bear an avalanche of memoranda, letters, cables and proofs—to say nothing of the daunting task of compressing into a few pages a great volume of law and practice and the experience of many years.

The laws of the territories covered by the contributors are stated as at 1st January, 1972.

London
14th January, 1972 MILTON GRUNDY

[4] For a discussion of the creation of settlements and family foundations in tax havens, see M. Grundy: *The Off-shore Trust*, 1972 British Tax Review, p. 336.

CONTENTS

		Page
PREFACE		5
BAHAMAS	Wobaco Trust Ltd., P.O. Box 100, Nassau, Bahamas.	13
BERMUDA	Bank of N. T. Butterfield & Son Ltd., Hamilton, Bermuda.	24
BRITISH VIRGIN ISLANDS	Tortola Trust Corporation Ltd., P.O. Box 69, Tortola, British Virgin Islands.	33
CAYMAN ISLANDS	Royal Bank Trust Company (Cayman) Ltd., P.O. Box 707, Grand Cayman, British West Indies.	39
GIBRALTAR	Gibraltar International Trust Corporation Ltd., Suite 1, Gibraltar Heights, Main Street, Gibraltar.	48
HONG KONG	The Chartered Bank Hong Kong Trustee Ltd., 4 and 4A Des Voeux Road Central, Hong Kong.	58
ISLE OF MAN	International Finance & Trust Corporation Ltd., P.O. Box 25, Douglas, Isle of Man.	71
JERSEY	Jersey International Bank of Commerce Ltd., 22 Hill Street, St. Helier, Jersey.	82
LIBERIA	The International Trust Company of Liberia, Monrovia, Liberia.	94
LIECHTENSTEIN	Allgemeines Treuunternehmen, P.O. Box 34.722, FL-9490 Vaduz, Liechtenstein.	102

		Page
LUXEMBOURG	Fiduciaire Générale de Luxembourg, 13 Bd de la Foire, Luxembourg.	119
NETHERLANDS ANTILLES	Curaçao International Trust Company N.V., 9B Handelsgade, Curaçao, Netherlands Antilles.	126
NEW HEBRIDES	Investors Trust Ltd., Port Vila, New Hebrides.	140
NORFOLK ISLAND	Permanent Trustee Company of Norfolk Island Ltd., Taylor's Road, Norfolk Island, South Pacific.	144
PANAMA	International Service Company Inc., Apartado 7440, Panama.	153
SWITZERLAND	Fleuri + Greutert Trust and Auditing Company Ltd., Member, Swiss Chamber of Auditing, Neustadthof, Mellingerstrasse 1, 5401 Baden, Switzerland.	162

GRUNDY'S TAX HAVENS

THE BAHAMAS

WOBACO TRUST LIMITED

The Bahamas is an archipelago of some 700 islands and innumerable cays and rocks lying between Haiti on the south-east and Florida on the north-west. Having a land mass of approximately 5,400 square miles, the Bahamas are set in some 70,000 square miles of clear blue sea and enjoy a fine year round climate which makes tourism the main industry. The sun shines on most days and the average monthly temperatures vary from 70°F. in February to 80°F. in August with a corresponding increase in relative humidity from 76 per cent to 82 per cent for the same months. June and October are generally the months when rainfall is heaviest, these two months normally accounting for half of the annual rainfall of approximately 50 inches based on a ten-year period up to 1966. The Bahamas has an estimated population of 170,000 of which 100,000 are estimated to live on New Providence, where the capital of the Bahamas, Nassau, is located.

Whilst tourism is the main industry, the complete absence of any form of taxation on income or capital gains has made the Bahamas into one of the most important locations in the world for investment companies and "offshore" companies, and the provision of banking and related financial services has now become the second largest industry in the Bahamas. The principal visible exports are pulpwood, cement, rum, salt, marine and agricultural products.

The economic expansion enjoyed by the Bahamas in the last few years can be attributed to its popularity both as a tourist resort and as a tax haven. Each year an increasing number of people benefit from the services which are available in the Bahamas.

In the free world, most businessmen strive to preserve and accumulate assets, whilst maximising the return generated by the prudent stewardship of those assets. This goal becomes harder to achieve as governments impose heavier taxation and more restrictive regulations in almost every sector of business and private life.

Assistance can be offered to a wide variety of people, from the popular entertainer, or author, whose income is basically derived from fees and royalties, the family businessman whose main concern will be the effect of estate duty or other administrative delays of probate on his estate, business or his personal holdings in the business, to the person whose capital is invested in marketable securities and whose main concern is the effect of capital gains and income tax on his portfolio. Furthermore, substantial benefits can accrue to multi-national corporations trading throughout the world, from the freedom encountered in using a holding or subsidiary company in the Bahamas to increase cash flow or accumulate profits offshore. Falling into these categories are those who can use the Bahamas to the best advantage, and many who come to Nassau for a period of relaxation in the sun return home with positive evidence of the opportunities to preserve their, their company's or their family's fortunes afforded by the Isles of Perpetual June.

Communications

There are regular air services from Nassau to London, New York, Toronto, Boston, Chicago, Miami, Jamaica, Bermuda and Luxembourg. Miami International Airport in Florida, which is only 35 minutes from Nassau by jet service, provides access to any other part of the world through scheduled international airlines. Frequent air services to the Out Islands are operated. There is also regular sea transport between Nassau and Miami or New York.

Government

The Commonwealth of the Bahamas is a self-governing British Colony; the Constitution of 1964 gave the country internal self-government, and this was extended by further measures in 1968. The Crown appoints the Governor of the Colony who is responsible for most matters concerning defence, internal security and foreign affairs.

Apart from these matters, the Colony is governed on a ministerial basis with an Upper and Lower chamber legislature. The Cabinet consists of the Premier and not less than eight ministers. The Senate (Upper House) has 16 members appointed by the Governor, 3 of whom are nominated by him, 9 by the Premier and 4 by the opposition leader. The House of Assembly (Lower House) is elected every five years by the people, and consists of thirty-eight members representing constituencies in Nassau and the Out Islands. Legislation must be passed by both the Senate and the House of Assembly, although the Senate may in certain circumstances delay legislation passed by the House of Assembly. The Governor must also give his assent to legislation on the advice of the Cabinet unless such legislation is contrary to the Bahamas Constitution, inconsistent with Treaty obligations for the British Government, or prejudicial for a defined reason.

The aims of the present government are stated to be:

a programme of social development projects;
an expanded economy through the encouragement of foreign investment;
the further expansion of tourism;
diversification of the economy by attracting light industry and developing agriculture and fisheries;
Bahamianization of the private and public sectors, which has been said not to indicate a desire for nationalization nor Government control, and furthermore the Government has expressly stated that it will not introduce income tax nor corporate tax.

Law

The law of the Bahamas is based on the British common law. The highest law court is the Court of Appeal presided over by three judges, usually leading jurists of England or West Indian nations. From the Court of Appeal there is also, in appropriate cases, the right of appeal to the Judicial Committee of the Privy Council in England.

The Supreme Court has general, civil and criminal jurisdiction. There are four Magistrates Courts in the Bahamas and in addition all Out Island Commissioners serve as Magistrates.

Language

English is the language of the Bahamas.

Currency and Exchange Control

Currency

The unit of currency was changed from the Bahamian pound sterling to the Bahamian dollar on the 25th May, 1966. The B.$ had a value of 7/- or approximately U.S. ·93¢. Following the devaluation of the British pound on the 18th November, 1967, the B.$ was revalued at 8s. 2d. to maintain its relationship to the U.S.$.

On the 2nd February, 1970 the B.$ was again revalued to parity with the U.S.$. Following the 1971 international currency re-alignments, the B.$ was devalued on the 24th December, 1971, only partly following the U.S.$ devaluation and is currently exchanged at approximately B.$2·50 to a Pound Sterling, or ·97¢ to U.S.$1·00. The Bahamian dollar is a currency of the Scheduled Territories. United States and Canadian dollars are generally accepted at a standard rate of exchange because of the country's reliance on revenue from tourists.

Exchange Control

The Bahamas, as part of the sterling area, has exchange control regulations which conform generally to the basic principles of the sterling area. Sterling transactions between the Bahamas and other countries in the sterling area now also generally require exchange control permission.

Although the Bahamas is a part of the sterling area, the Bahamas Government has exercised control over exchange operations for the past thirty years. The Bahamas Exchange Control does however consult the Bank of England on broader matters of principle concerning exchange restrictions, and most resident individuals and companies deal generally in a sterling currency. Exchange control, however, has endeavoured in recent years to facilitate the commercial and investment transactions of individuals temporarily resident in the Bahamas, and more importantly, companies owned and trusts formed by persons living in countries outside the sterling area or carrying on commercial or investment activities entirely outside the sterling area.

Resident Status

Companies or trusts are classified by exchange control as resident when trading or investing within the sterling area. Normally, resident companies will operate through resident sterling accounts. Receipts of external sterling and dollars converted at the ruling rate, would be credited to resident sterling account. As resident companies cannot make payments from resident sterling account to external sterling or foreign currency account without specific consent, the permission of exchange control is required before dividends convertible into foreign currency can be paid, or loans made to a foreign parent or associated company from net income. Where however, the majority of a resident company's shareholders are resident overseas and not specifically inside the sterling area, permission is readily given for the distribution of profits by a properly declared dividend. On liquidation, the repatriation from resident sterling account to foreign shareholders of the proceeds on disposal of a resident company's net assets, in the form of foreign currencies will require consent.

Where however, the original capital investment was in dollars, as in the case of a resident company owned by a United States organization, capital may be repatriated in dollars on liquidation provided that "approved status" was obtained at the time of the formation of the company.

Under certain circumstances, a "resident" company may operate a foreign currency account with permission from exchange control where it can show that the nature of its business is such that the company's operations would be hindered without the ability to maintain such an account. Exchange control will normally require that the company obtaining this special permission keep the Authority informed of transactions over such an account.

An individual who is normally resident outside the sterling area but who is temporarily resident in the Bahamas may, with exchange control approval, maintain his home currency account without converting this currency into resident sterling. He may also claim exemption from having to bring income from his home currency assets to the Bahamas for conversion to a sterling account.

Non-resident Status

This is the classification given to individuals, companies or trusts whose trade or investment is entirely outside the sterling area. Once non-resident status has been granted, transactions involving negotiable foreign securities may be carried out without further approval from exchange control. Dollar bank accounts may be maintained in the Bahamas, the United States or elsewhere. While many non-resident companies operate resident sterling accounts in order to pay local suppliers, salaries and establishment expenses, these resident sterling accounts may not be credited with the occasional receipts of resident sterling. Resident sterling received by non-resident entities cannot be deposited or converted into dollars. Where a non-resident company trades with persons or companies located inside the sterling area, the customer must apply for exchange control permission to pay external sterling or dollars to the non-resident company.

Non-residents may with the prior approval of exchange control purchase Bahamian real property as an "approved investment". The purchaser is assured that he will be able to repatriate the sales proceeds at a later date in his own currency.

Citizens of the United States and Canada may, subject to the restrictions imposed by their own country, enter and leave the Bahamas with unlimited amounts of dollar travel funds and may also obtain permission for earned income arising in the Bahamas to be credited to dollar accounts inside or outside the Bahamas.

Before goods are exported to the Bahamas, it is essential that an import licence is obtained by the importing company or individual in order that foreign exchange will be made available.

Financial and Professional Services

The Bahamas' unique tax laws have made the country one of the established financial centres of the Western world. Many of the largest international commercial banks are represented in Nassau and Freeport, and supplementing their services are the trust companies, equipped to handle a wide range of financial operations and provide responsible management. As would be expected, there is no shortage of skilled professional advisers in the Bahamas. The leading international firms of accountants are represented in Nassau and Freeport. There are highly skilled lawyers, investment advisers and stockbrokers in the Bahamas capable of providing their services and experience in connection with all legal and financial matters.

Specific advantages derived from banking in the Bahamas are as follows:

(*a*) investors can make deposits in any freely convertible currency and interest is payable without deduction of withholding tax although exchange control permission may be required in certain instances;

(*b*) depositors are not required to pay custody fees as they do in some countries, and interest rates on term deposits are competitive;

(*c*) only by obtaining an order by the Supreme Court can an outsider force a Bahamian financial institution to release any confidential information concerning the status of a customer's account;

(*d*) the deposits of deceased persons are not subject to estate, death or inheritance taxes, and are usually easier to withdraw by a personal representative than in most countries.

Apart from the commercial, merchant and Eurodollar banks, there are a number of savings and loan institutions and established unit trusts and mutual funds which give investors the opportunity of investing in United States and other foreign securities through a Bahamian company.

Internal Tax Structure

There are no personal income taxes, profit taxes, corporation or capital gains taxes in the Bahamas, nor are there estate or inheritance taxes. The only tax levied is a real property tax based on the value of improved property on the island of New Providence.

The revenues of the Bahamian government derive principally from taxes on imports, stamp duties and certain business licence fees, together with the tax imposed on the casinos operating in the Bahamas.

Certain specific tax exemptions and industrial incentives are available for the encouragement of hotels and light industries and a tax-free zone has been established on the island of Grand Bahama. The Grand Bahama Port Authority Limited has guaranteed licensees within the Freeport area, freedom from taxes on income, capital gains, real estate and personal property for a period of 35 years commencing from August 1955. For a period of 99 years from the same date, licensees are guaranteed freedom from customs duties (except on imports for personal use or consumption), excise taxes and stamp duties.

Stamp Duties

All monies remitted abroad from the Bahamas, except where remitted from Freeport or from bank accounts maintained outside the Bahamas, are subject to a stamp tax.

Certain documents require to be stamped. Some carry fixed duties (of modest amounts); others are stampable *ad valorem* (but subject to minimum amounts and sliding scales)—*e.g.* deeds, mortgages, debentures and authorized share capital.

Dividends and Interest Paid

There is no withholding tax on dividends and term payments arising from assets held in the Bahamas. However, the status of the recipient, *i.e.* whether resident or non-resident for exchange control purposes, is an important factor in determining whether funds may be physically transferred out of the Bahamas without exchange control permission.

Licence Fees

During 1969, measures were introduced which provide for the payment of an annual licence fee by banks and trust companies registered in the Bahamas which includes the local branches of foreign banks. The annual fee varies from B.$30,000 for a full commercial bank licence to B.$1,500 for a private bank providing limited services.

Tax Treaties

Income received in the Bahamas from investments abroad may be subject to withholding taxes in the country where such income originates. Before investing abroad, therefore, a Bahamian company, trust or individual should examine the withholding regulations of the country concerned. No double taxation agreements have been concluded between the Bahamas and any other country.

Available Entities

The most popular business entities used in the Bahamas are companies having limited liability, trusts and settlements. To a lesser extent partnerships, branches and sole traders are established forms of trading.

There is no specific legislation governing the conduct of a business by a sole trader apart from the Immigration Laws which require that any non-Bahamian person must be in possession of a work permit before engaging in any kind of gainful employment in the Bahamas.

The Company

Generally speaking a person from outside the Bahamas will arrange for the incorporation of a Bahamian company to conduct business in the Colony, although a foreign company can open a branch in the Bahamas without registering it, unless it is intended that the branch should own property or enter into any property leasing arrangements. Under these circumstances, the branch would require to be registered under the Foreign Companies Act and pay an initial stamp duty of approximately B.$600.

Statutory requirements to be fulfilled in incorporating a Bahamian company are laid down in the Companies Act 1866 as amended by the Companies Amendment Act 1965.

Generally, incorporation is handled by a Bahamian lawyer who prepares the memorandum and articles of association in the form which best suits the nature of a particular company's business. Although the Companies Act states that a company must have a minimum of five shareholders, they can be of any nationality. The memorandum of a company limited by shares must contain the following information:

(*a*) the part of the Colony in which the registered office is to be located;
(*b*) the objects for which the proposed company is to be established;
(*c*) a declaration that the liability of the members is limited, and
(*d*) the share capital of the company.

Stamp duty is payable on the filing of the memorandum and articles of association.

Until the Companies Amendment Act 1965, the share capital of a Bahamian company could not be reduced, nor could there be any repayment of capital to shareholders other than on liquidation. The new Act provides that companies may now issue bearer shares, reduce share capital on the authority of the Court subject to specific legislation embodied in the Act for the protection of creditors, and may now issue redeemable preference shares.

The articles of association usually state the number of directors to be appointed. There are no restrictions on the nationality of directors, although for convenience it is customary to appoint local residents. Where permitted by the articles of association, directors' or shareholders' meetings may be held anywhere in the world. Alternate directors may be appointed and attendance at meetings may be by proxy.

Statutory records to be kept by Bahamian companies include registers of directors and members, and minute books. Annual returns must also be filed with the Registrar of Companies, giving information concerning shareholders, directors and officers, the registered office, and share capital.

Bahamian companies are not required by law to have auditors, nor is there any requirement, except in the case of banks and trust companies, for the filing of audited financial statements with the Registrar. The statutory records of all companies must be kept at each company's registered office. The location of the registered office must be recorded with the Registrar General, advertised in the official Gazette and the company's name must be displayed on a sign attached to the building where the registered office is located.

The cost of incorporating a Bahamian company is usually in the region of B.$1,100 which includes the statutory filing fee of B.$290 and incorporation takes only a few days. The annual maintenance costs for directors' fees, management and other expenses will vary depending upon the amount of time involved in operating the company, and will range from B.$250 for a small company to several thousand for a company transacting a substantial amount of business. Additionally, all companies are required to pay an annual registration fee of B.$250.

Apart from the advantages of favourable exchange control status already mentioned, there can be considerable tax savings in the use of a company based in the Bahamas. Revenue collected in the Bahamas may not have been paid under deduction of income or withholding tax. There are no taxes on the profits of the Bahamian entity, and so one can accelerate the accumulation of profits to be used, for example, for reinvestment in capital projects, fleet replacement or insurance reserves.

The Trust

Bahamian trusts are in most respects similar to trusts which can be created under English law, the most significant difference being that income may be accumulated for the whole of the "perpetuity period". A trust company is generally appointed as sole trustee and given wide powers as regards investment of the fund and for the ultimate distribution of the fund among the beneficiaries, although these powers may of course be circumscribed and made subject to such consents or vetoes as the settlor may desire. The ideal to be aimed at is to have the powers of the trustee wide enough to deal with all possible future circumstances whilst ensuring that the ultimate benefit of the fund enures to the persons for whom the grantor or settlor wishes to provide.

It is often both convenient and advantageous, where the trust funds are to be invested in the U.S., or other high-tax country, for the trustee to incorporate one or more investment companies for the purpose. But this is a difficult area in which it is impossible to generalize, and the drafting of the trust and the investment strategy of the trustee are matters upon which the intending grantor or settlor will require specialist advice.

The Partnership

These may be formed by an association of individuals, companies or both, and may include limited or general partners. Where limited partners are present in the entity, there are regulations laid down by the Partnership Limited Liability Act which states, *inter alia*, that:

(1) the word limited must appear at the end of the firm's name;
(2) the limited partners may not conduct any of the business of the partners;
(3) a duly executed partnership agreement must be filed with the Registrar.

Limited partners are liable for the debts of the partnership only to the extent of their capital contributions to the partnership.

BERMUDA

BANK OF N. T. BUTTERFIELD AND SON LIMITED

Bermuda is a British Colony and has the oldest colonial bicameral legislature in the Commonwealth, excluding the Parliament at Westminster. It occupies a geographical position that has made it a natural centre for business activities of increasing importance in many spheres. Its historical growth shows an ability to adapt itself by constitutional methods to changing world conditions and Bermuda is in a position to maintain its place as a progressive independent and stable community.

Bermuda is situated some 560 miles east-south-east of Cape Hatteras, North Carolina, U.S.A. The Island group, with a population of nearly 52,000, comprises an archipelago of several hundred islets amongst seven principal, bridge-connected islands, and has a total land area of slightly over 20½ square miles, including two U.S. naval bases. Because of the Gulf Stream which separates the Colony from the North American Continent, Bermuda boasts one of the most delightful climates in the world; temperatures range from 56 degrees in the winter to 85 degrees in the summer. The islands are hilly with a maximum elevation of 260 feet above sea level. There are no forests but the soil does support a variety of bushes, trees, and a proliferation of vivid floral growth.

Communications

Because of its convenient mid-Atlantic geographical position, Bermuda offers an excellent world-wide communications system. The principal North American cities and security markets are within a few hours by air. The colony is served by six international airlines and there are direct flights to such places as London, New York, Montreal, Boston, Washington, Miami, Nassau, Jamaica, Trinidad, Bogota, Mexico City, Sydney, and Halifax. Jet flying time to New York is less than two hours and to London approximately 6½ hours. There are frequent steamship services for both passengers and freight to and from New York and other Eastern seaboard ports. Bermuda is also on the shipping routes between many United States, Canadian, and Northern European ports, as well as the Caribbean, South America, and Oceania. Cable, telex, and telephone facilities are excellent.

Government

Bermuda is a self-governing colony, whose new Constitution came into force in June 1968, following a General Election in May of that year. Under it the Colony moved over to a "responsible" cabinet form of Government complete with political parties.

The Executive authority of Bermuda is vested in Her Majesty and exercised on her behalf by the Governor and Commander-in-Chief appointed by her to hold office during her pleasure. Reserved for his personal discretion are responsibilities affecting external affairs, defence (including armed forces), internal security and police. Otherwise the Governor is advised by an Executive Council which is collectively responsible to the Legislature for any advice given to him for anything done under the authority of any Member of Executive Council in the execution of his office.

Although Bermuda is fully responsible for her internal domestic affairs, in diplomatic and consular representation, certain treaties and international conventions and the like, Great Britain still acts on behalf of the Colony.

No taxes are paid by Bermuda to Great Britain, nor in turn does Bermuda receive from her any grant-in-aid or other subsidy. The salaries of all Government servants including the Governor are paid by Bermuda out of its own revenue. The high standard of living promises a stable social and political base and a prosperous middle class for many years to come.

Law

Bermuda Law comprises the English common law and doctrines of equity, and the English Acts of general application which were in force at the date the Colony was settled in 1612, all as modified or added to by Bermuda statute law. The Courts in Bermuda consist of a Magistrate's Court, a Supreme Court and a Court of Appeal. Appeal lies from the Supreme Court to the Court of Appeals for Bermuda and thence to the Privy Council in England.

Language

The language of Bermuda is English.

Currency and Exchange Control

Bermuda is within the overall framework of the sterling area but has its own autonomous Foreign Exchange Control. The Control assigns a "designation" which is mainly based on the beneficial ownership of the Bermuda entity. The Control does not rule on strictly hypothetical cases but, for an example of its usual classifying process, one may consider the case of a Bermuda company funded in U.S. dollars and entirely owned by U.S. citizens and conducting its operations altogether outside the sterling area: such a company would be designated "external" or "non-resident". Provided that neither the operations nor ownership changed materially, it would be permitted to deal freely with its dollar and other external assets through a local bank. The basic consideration in all cases presented is whether there would be a net drain on the sterling area's foreign currency reserves or, on balance, any other inexpedient economic drawback. Individuals or legal entities resident outside the sterling area are not subject to exchange control over their non-sterling activities, and may deal directly with a bank without applying for "designation" or permission.

Capital invested in Bermuda by non-residents in projects that will directly benefit the economy of the Island, as approved by the Foreign Exchange Control, may be repatriated at any time thereafter together with the profit or interest realized from the investment. This concession applies to a non-resident who makes an investment in a foreign currency in Bermuda, provided the foreign currency is converted into local sterling. Application must be made to the Control for approval at the time the investment is being made.

It is always possible to obtain a ruling from the Control before the non-resident entity is formed and almost all bona fide problems arising are capable of a perfectly satisfactory solution involving the minimum of restriction.

For companies, partnerships, or individuals with "external" designation, capital is credited in the currency received. Income is credited in U.S. or Canadian Dollars as received, or if received in other currencies is normally carried in U.S. Dollars. Income from companies, partnerships or individuals designated "resident of the sterling area" by Bermuda's Foreign Exchange Control, is converted into or retained in sterling.

Financial and Professional Services

Banks in Bermuda offer a comprehensive range of commercial banking facilities. They are in correspondence with leading financial institutions in the major cities around the world and are equipped to provide all services usually rendered by a corporate trustee. Accounts may be maintained in Bermuda, United States, and Canadian Dollars, and in Pounds Sterling.

Joint accounts with the right of survivorship are legal under Bermuda Law and on the death of one or more of the joint holders, legal title to the assets in the account passes to the survivors without further formality since there are no death or estate duties in Bermuda. Any joint single holder (including a minor) may sign against the account individually.

On the death of the ultimate survivor, however, the assets can only be released to his executor under a properly executed will proved before a court of competent jurisdiction, or under the law of intestacy. The necessity for making a Bermuda will (which is a matter of public record) can be avoided by forming a simple Bermuda trust (see below) which contains directions for the custody or distribution of the property settled in the trust after the death of the settlor.

Audit and full accounting facilities are available through chartered accountants, several of whom are associated with international firms. Qualified technical personnel for office and other work may be introduced to Bermuda subject to the permission in each case of the Department of Immigration. There is, however, a reasonable amount of literate semi-skilled and unskilled labour available locally.

Normally the local law firms, who act as incorporating attorneys, provide the head office and corporate secretary whose services include calling of meetings of shareholders and directors, maintenance of minute books, stock registers and other statutory records. It is also normal for one or more of the partners to act as directors.

Internal Tax Structure

There is virtually no taxation in direct form; no income tax, capital gains, excess profits, dividend, gift, inheritance tax, and no estate duty. Bermuda has no tax treaties with other countries covering mutual reductions of withholding tax, tax credits or exchange of fiscal information. There is a small land tax of less than 1 per cent on assessed value levied by each of the nine parish vestries for parochial purposes; there is also a minimal property levy imposed by the central Government which is based on 10 per cent of the assessed rental value of land and dwellings.

Although measures to implement an income tax have been before the Legislature in the past, they have been rejected. In any event, such bills provided exemption from the tax for non-Bermudians more than 90 per cent of whose income originated from outside the Island, even when such persons resided locally the year round. Moreover, by an Act passed in 1966, which extended an earlier Act, the Legislature empowered the Executive to give to a Bermuda corporation or partnership owned abroad a guarantee of exemption from certain direct taxes which may in the future be imposed. These guarantees are effective to the end of March 1996.

Government revenue is derived largely from *ad valorem* import duties, land assessments, and to a lesser extent from miscellaneous departmental receipts such as pilotage, vehicle licensing, postage stamp duties and exempted company fees (mentioned later). These exempted company fees constitute the principal direct benefit the Bermuda Government itself gains from the incorporation of local companies by foreign interests. Obviously, however, there are also many indirect benefits to the Island's economy through banks, merchants, public utilities, hotels, and the like.

The Bermuda Government has no foreign Public Debt and only a small local debt which is in part covered by the Reserve Fund. The Note Security Fund is an additional reserve covering the Bermuda Government note issue in excess of 100 per cent.

Freeport

In 1954 Bermuda purchased from the Imperial Government certain Crown Lands including the H.M. Dockyard which was declared a freeport by the Legislature in 1956. A number of well-known firms are conducting light industrial operations from this site which has two deep water shipping basins with extensive loading, unloading, bunkering and warehouse facilities.

Available Entities

These may be considered under three headings: companies; partnerships and trusts.

The Company

Until the beginning of 1970 August all limited liability companies in Bermuda were incorporated by private Acts of the Bermuda Legislature. With the passing of the Companies (Incorporation by Registration) Act 1970, however, a new procedure was introduced which enables companies to be incorporated without petitioning the Legislature. It is still possible to incorporate under the old system if the promoters so wish. The new system makes it possible to incorporate more quickly, and also to change the powers of a company without going back to the Legislature.

Bermuda companies fall into two main classes. The first class is of companies incorporated by local businessmen to trade in Bermuda, and are referred to in the statutes as "local companies". The other class comprises companies incorporated by non-Bermudians to conduct business outside Bermuda from a head office in Bermuda; these companies are called "exempted companies". Exempted companies are so called because they are exempted from those provisions of the companies statute law which restricts the proportion of share capital which may be held by aliens.

Exempted companies are restricted by statute from holding mortgages on land in Bermuda, from acquiring bonds or debentures secured on any such land, from acquiring shares issued by or any interest in any local company or business and from trading or doing business with persons in Bermuda except in furtherance of their business carried on outside Bermuda. There are, however, exceptional cases in which an exempted company engaged in manufacturing or processing may be authorized to sell a portion of its product to local retailers; each particular case requesting some relaxation in the general restrictions is judged on its own merits. No exempted company may own Bermuda land without the express authorization of the local Legislature.

Profits can be accumulated and it is not obligatory to pay dividends: the only "tax" imposed on an exempted company (other than a nominal stamp duty on the authorized capital of the company, see *infra*) is an annual government fee of $480. The first payment of $480 is made immediately on incorporation and subsequent payments are made in January of each year. If a company is incorporated after the 31st August in any year then its tax for the remainder of the year will be $240 instead of $480.

There is a stamp duty of one-quarter of 1 per cent on the authorized capital of a company, and this is paid when the company is incorporated. Stamp duty at the same rate is payable on any increased share capital. Stamp duty is payable on mortgages, debentures and bonds at the rate of one-fifth of 1 per cent and on conveyances and share transfers at the rate of one-half of 1 per cent. In the case of sales of bonded precious stones there is a sales tax of one-half of 1 per cent.

While the company's share capital must be fully subscribed, it need not be fully paid up. As a matter of policy the Legislature requires that the minimum share capital of an exempted company be not less than $12,000.

A Bermuda company can own and operate ships: if a ship is registered in Bermuda (annual fee $240) it qualifies as a "British Ship" for most of the purposes of the Imperial Merchant Shipping Act 1894.

The Trust

A Bermuda trust has a form very similar to that which is found in other territories whose laws are based on the English common law and equity. The income of the trust fund may be accumulated throughout the whole of the "perpetuity period".

A trust in respect of which any of the beneficiaries are non-Bermudians cannot own Bermuda land without the permission of the Governor-in-Council. The amount of land available for non-Bermudian ownership is limited, and hence the Governor-in-Council does not look favourably on large holdings by non-Bermudians. There is nothing in Bermuda Law to prevent foreign land from being part of a trust fund. Naturally, reference should be made to the law of the country where such land is situated before transferring it to the trust.

A Bermuda trust may be formed with only one trustee if the settlor so wishes, and in this connection the banks in Bermuda provide a full range of corporate trustee services.

A trust document bears stamp duty at the rate of one-quarter of 1 per cent of the capital value of the trust fund at the date of the creation of the trust. Further stamp duty at the same rate is payable in respect of additional property subsequently transferred to the trustee as an accretion to the trust fund. Where the trust document directs that income be accumulated and added to the trust fund as an accretion, no stamp duty is payable on any such accretion.

In the case of a discretionary trust under which the trustee is given a power of appointment, stamp duty in the amount of $2·40 is payable in respect of each appointment, no matter how large such appointment may be.

The Partnership

As in the case of companies, Bermuda partnerships fall into two main classes: those formed by Bermudians to trade locally and those formed by non-Bermudians to conduct business outside Bermuda. Partnerships of the latter class are known as "exempted partnerships", and it is with these that this chapter is concerned.

Exempted partnerships may be divided into two classes, namely, ordinary partnerships and limited partnerships. Persons forming a limited partnership must sign a certificate containing the firm name, the names and addresses of the partners (distinguishing general partners from special partners), the amount of capital stock each special partner has contributed, the general nature of the business to be transacted, and the time when the partnership is to commence and terminate. This certificate is filed in the Registry and is open to public inspection. In addition, a copy of the certificate must be published once in the local newspaper for the time being designated as the Official Gazette.

A partnership carries on business subject to the provisions of its articles of partnership and to the general partnership statute law of Bermuda. The general statutes are the Partnership Act 1902, the Limited Partnership Act 1883, and the Exempted Partnerships Act 1958.

Exempted partnerships are restricted by the Exempted Partnerships Act 1958 from doing business with anyone in Bermuda except in relation to any contract or agreement which is to be wholly performed outside Bermuda. In addition, the Act prohibits exempted partnerships from engaging in commercial banking or merchant banking business in Bermuda. The Exempted Partnerships Act expressly provides that exempted partnerships shall transact all banking business conducted in Bermuda with and through one of the local banks.

The Act does not prevent such partnerships from acquiring or dealing in goods bona fide required by the partnership for the administration of its business offices in Bermuda, nor does the Act prevent the registration by such partnerships of patents, trade marks and copyrights in Bermuda.

An exempted partnership is formed by the partners executing articles of partnership. The articles of partnership of an exempted partnership must be registered with the Registrar General. Before registration, the articles of partnership must be submitted to the Department of Immigration for the approval of the names of the partners, the nature of the business to be carried on by them and the amount of the capital of the partnership. Before granting its approval the Department of Immigration is obliged to consult with the Foreign Exchange Control.

An exempted partnership may not carry on any business in Bermuda unless within one month after registration a certificate of registration is produced to the Accountant General and a tax of $480 is paid into the Public Treasury. In January of each year subsequent to its formation an exempted partnership must pay into the public Treasury an additional sum of $480.

The articles of partnership must contain details of the nature of the business to be undertaken by the partnership, and the partnership may not undertake any business which is not specified in its articles. Further, the articles of partnership may not be altered without the prior approval of the Department of Immigration. It is possible for an exempted partnership to have one or more partners who are resident in Bermuda. However, it is essential that at least one of the partners shall be a non-Bermudian.

Every exempted partnership is obliged to maintain an office and a resident manager in Bermuda and to keep at this office such audited accounts and records as will show the business of the partnership and a true accounting thereof at the end of each financial year.

Stamp duty is payable on the articles of partnership at the rate of one-quarter of 1 per cent of the amount of the capital to be contributed. In the case of any increase in the contributed capital, stamp duty is payable at the same rate.

THE BRITISH VIRGIN ISLANDS

THE TORTOLA TRUST CORPORATION LIMITED

The British Virgin Islands which form the north-western extremity of the Leeward Islands are located some 60 miles east of Puerto Rico. There are over 60 islands, with a total land area of 69 square miles, but only 16 of them are inhabited. The most important is Tortola (21 square miles), Virgin Gorda (8·3 square miles), Jost Van Dyke (3·5 square miles) and Anegada (15 square miles). The American islands of St. Thomas, St. John and St. Croix form part of the same archipelago and, because of their proximity, the two groups have strong economic and social ties.

With the exception of Anegada which is a flat coral island consisting almost entirely of limestone with very little subsoil, the Islands are hilly and very picturesque. Together with the American islands, they form probably the finest sailing area in the world. The waters are rich in gamefish and off Anegada there are said to lie more than 400 wrecks, most of them on the reef which extends southwards towards Virgin Gorda.

The Islands enjoy a particularly healthy climate, sub-tropical but with the extreme heats moderated by the trade winds. The average annual rainfall at Road Town, the capital, on the south-east of Tortola is 49 inches. The average temperature in winter is 71° to 82°F., seldom dropping below 67°, and in summer 78° to 88°. Hurricanes are rare, the last occurrence being in 1928.

The low tax rates enjoyed by the British Virgin Islands, their social and political stability and their freedom from exchange control (although part of the sterling area), are factors which together have attracted a substantial amount of off-shore business to the Territory. Government is in principle in favour of the development of the Islands as a financial centre and a number of international operations are finding a sympathetic and profitable home there.

Communications

The airport is on Beef Island, which is connected to Tortola by the Queen Elizabeth II bridge, 10 miles east of Road Town. L.I.A.T.

(Leeward Islands Air Transport) operates a daily service to Antigua (with connections to London) and to St. Thomas and Puerto Rico (with connections to New York and other American cities). Prinair (Puerto Rican International Airlines) and other smaller companies operate frequent daily services to St. Thomas and Puerto Rico and to neighbouring islands. There is also a boat service (45 minutes) daily between West End, Tortola and St. Thomas.

Various shipping companies operate direct services from the United Kingdom, continental Europe and the United States.

An excellent internal telephone service is operated by Cable and Wireless who also offer external cable, radio telephone and telex services to all parts of the world.

Government

The Governor is Her Majesty's representative and, under the 1967 Constitution, is responsible for external affairs, defence, the judicial and legal departments of government, internal security and civil service and finance. On other matters, he is normally bound to act in accordance with the advice of the Executive Council, which is comprised of the Governor as Chairman, two ex-officio members (the Attorney General and Financial Secretary), the Chief Minister and two other ministers appointed by the Governor on the advice of the Chief Minister.

The Legislative Council consists of a Speaker chosen from outside the Council, the two ex-officio members of the Executive Council, one nominated member appointed by the Governor and seven elected members, one from each of seven electoral districts.

There was a general election in June 1971, and the Governor appointed the Hon. W. Wheatley as Chief Minister.

Law

The Law of the British Virgin Islands is based on the British common law. Income arising under trusts can be accumulated for the whole of the "perpetuity period". There are restrictions on land ownership which affect persons who are not what are called "belongers" in the Territory.

Language

The Language of the Territory is English.

Currency and Exchange Control

The British Virgin Islands are a part of the sterling area although the U.S. dollar is the every day currency in use in the Islands and is the only legal tender. Residents of the British Virgin Islands may operate dollar accounts and sterling accounts; they apply to the Bank of England to convert sterling (other than external sterling) into dollars. Traditionally, the Islands have always used the currency in circulation in the neighbouring U.S. Virgin Islands. The economic ties between the two communities are very close and it is this fact which is responsible for the anomalous position of the British Virgin Islands—a territory which for all practical purposes is both inside and outside the sterling area.

A holder of internal sterling who wishes to invest capital in the Islands will first apply to the Governor through a bank in the Islands. The application bearing the Governor's recommendation is then forwarded to the Exchange Control Authorities in the country from which the sterling will be remitted. Two examples may make the approved procedure clear:

(1) Smith, a resident in Eire, wishes to buy property in the B.V.I. from a resident of the Islands named Lettsome. The price is agreed for conversion of the sterling equivalent of $20,000. The Governor recommends the conversion and the Bank of England approves. Smith remits sterling to Lettsome by cheque which Lettsome then converts into dollars through his bank.

(2) Jones, who is a resident of the United Kingdom, wishes to form a B.V.I. company called Jones Hotels Limited for the purpose of building and operating a hotel. Capital is required to build the hotel and operate it for the first season. Jones Hotels Limited will apply through a bank in the B.V.I. for conversion of sterling for the capitalization of the Company giving full details of the project and the approximate timing of the conversion. Jones will be required to give an undertaking to the Bank of England that he will not, without the Bank's approval, part with the shares he has thus acquired nor will he dispose of any dividends other than by the sale to an authorized dealer in the United Kingdom.

As far as sterling area residents are concerned, shares in B.V.I. companies which are denominated in U.S. dollars or other non-sterling currency are non-sterling assets, but because the B.V.I. are in the Scheduled Territories, such shares may be acquired without payment of the investment currency premium. They may also be reconverted into sterling when sold without any deduction. Property in the British Virgin Islands is similarly treated: it may be acquired by direct sterling to dollar conversion without having to purchase premium dollars. These factors alone have been of tremendous importance to the Islands and they are to a large extent responsible for the influx of sterling capital into development projects in the B.V.I.

Financial and Professional Services

World wide banking facilities are available through four commercial banks, and the accountancy and legal professions are well represented.

Internal Tax Structure

The rates of income tax are as under:

companies—12 per cent on chargeable income;
individuals—3 per cent on total income and 12 per cent on balance of total income after deduction of personal and other allowances.

In the case of residents, tax is chargeable on world income whether received in the Territory or not with the exception of earned income:

(*a*) arising from the U.S. Virgin Islands and Puerto Rico, which is exempt; and
(*b*) from elsewhere, which is taxable on the amount received in the territory.

In the case of persons not domiciled or not ordinarily resident in the British Virgin Islands, the tax is restricted to the income received in the Territory. Tax is not payable on the external income of a temporary resident or one who has not resided in the territory for at least six months of the year for which he is being assessed.

There are no taxes on capital wealth or capital gains, and no sales taxes or death duties. Import duties range from a preferential rate of 8 per cent to 15 per cent to a general rate of 12 per cent to 24 per cent plus a surcharge of 20 per cent of the duty.

Stamp duty of 35 cents is payable on a bill of exchange, but none on a cheque or banker's draft.

On a conveyance or transfer of real estate, shares or other property the duty is 2·5 per cent of the value (with a sliding scale below $250).

Under the Pioneer Services and Hotels Aid legislation, generous tax concessions are available to investors. The Pioneer Services Ordinance provides incentive to investors to develop or establish services and industries needed by the Territory and a tax holiday period of up to ten years can be claimed by such approved industries. Under the Hotels Aid Ordinance, hotels containing not more than 9 bedrooms are allowed a tax holiday of up to 10 years, and those containing 10 bedrooms or more, 20 years.

Tax Treaties

Double Taxation Agreements exist between the British Virgin Islands and the United Kingdom, Denmark, Norway, Sweden, Switzerland and the U.S.A., and unilateral relief is given on income derived from other Commonwealth countries. The Agreement with the United Kingdom terminated with the British Virgin Islands tax year 1971 and the United Kingdom Tax year ended 5th April, 1972. At the time of going to press, it had been reported that the terms of the new Agreement had been settled but no details were available.

Available Entities

The Company

The Territory's Companies Ordinance was passed in 1885 and is modelled on the British legislation of that time. Companies may be registered with the capital expressed in dollars or in a currency other than dollars. Registration can be speedily effected and the documentation required is minimal. The statutory annual maintenance costs, apart from a trade licence should it be required, are negligible.

The Trust

In general, trust income is charged to tax and in some circumstances the settlor or grantor may himself be liable. However, it is not the practice to tax trust income where all the beneficiaries reside outside the Territory.

The Partnership

Income earned by a partnership is declared as such but each partner is liable individually for his share of the income.

CAYMAN ISLANDS

ROYAL BANK TRUST COMPANY (CAYMAN) LIMITED

475 miles south from Miami and about 200 miles north-west from Montego Bay lies possibly the best and most advantageous tax haven for foreign investors—the British Crown Colony of the Cayman Islands.

There are three islands in the group: George Town, the capital and major business and financial centre, is located on the largest island, Grand Cayman, 22 miles long and 76 square miles in area; Cayman Brac, some 90 miles to the east, has an area of 14 square miles; Little Cayman, 5 miles west of "the Brac", is only 10 square miles. The climate is tropical, typical of the Caribbean, but tempered by the trade winds.

A Cayman legend—based on history, though not on legal fact—attributes the tax-free status of the Islands to an act of courage by the Caymanian people almost two hundred years ago. In 1798, during a great storm, as they tell it, sailing ships were wrecked, one after another, on the barrier reef at Gun Bay at the eastern end of Grand Cayman. Wise in the ways of the sea, islanders braved the surf in rescue, and all lives were saved. Among the rescued were two distinguished personages, a British prince and his protector, an admiral. When they returned to England and told George III of their rescue, the monarch decreed that the Caymanians would be free forever from taxation and war-time conscription.

The story may be apocryphal, but it is a fact that, to this day, the Cayman Islands remain tax-free in a heavily taxed world.

Until a short while ago the Islands were probably the least well known of the currently popular tax havens. Recently, however, their popularity has been growing rapidly. The Government values the increasing revenues from those seeking shelter from heavy taxation, and realizes that if this growth is to continue, it must ensure both that services are as good and effective as in other areas and that the cost of those services is economically attractive.

Up-to-date, business-orientated legislation, political stability and good communications have encouraged banks, trust companies, lawyers and accountants to extend and improve their facilities. Government regulations are favourable. Government legal fees are moderate. Government policy is aimed at maintaining this situation. In the words of the Governor, the Cayman Islands are "a harbour for peace, stability and tax freedom". It is clearly the Caymanians' intention to keep things that way.

Communications

The Islands are at present served by two airlines: Cayman Airways Ltd., and L.A.C.S.A., flying Rolls-Royce-powered B.A.C. 111 jet aircraft. Their schedules provide ample flights to and from Miami; Kingston, Jamaica and San Jose, Costa Rica.

Negotiations are taking place with two other major airlines, and it is hoped that, as soon as the airport runway has been extended to accommodate the larger type of jet aircraft, these lines will also provide service to Grand Cayman.

Air-mail services are good, and telephone, telex and cable services are available via Cable and Wireless (West Indies) Ltd. The latter company is currently investing some £5½ million in additional facilities, aimed at providing improved reception and an increased number of international lines.

Government

The Cayman Islands were formerly a dependency of Jamaica. In 1962, however, when Jamaica became independent, they elected to remain a Crown Colony—and still appear contented with this arrangement, as none of the political parties, or indeed any other organized group, is seeking independence or other form of complete self-government.

Her Majesty is represented locally by a Governor appointed by the Crown, who is assisted by an Executive Council consisting of nominated members from the elected Legislative Assembly. There is universal adult suffrage for all British subjects resident in the Islands.

The population of approximately 11,000 is by origin 20 per cent European, 20 per cent African and 60 per cent mixed parentage. There appear to be no signs of racial unrest or political instability, and the

Government is actively encouraging the development of a tourist industry.

Law

The law is basically English common law.

Language

The language of the Islands is English.

Currency and Exchange Control

The Cayman Islands are in the Scheduled Territories (sometimes called the sterling area). The present currency of the Islands is the Jamaica dollar, a sterling currency associated with the British pound. There are plans to introduce a national Cayman Islands currency in May 1972. This will remain a sterling currency but will be quoted on a par with the U.S. Dollar.

Exchange Control is administered by the Cayman Islands Exchange Controller; a local Government Civil Servant who operates under the Exchange Control law of the Cayman Islands.

Citizens of countries outside the sterling area, and Cayman Islands companies owned by such persons and not carrying on business in the sterling area, may be designated as "non-resident for exchange control". Non-residents are granted complete freedom from the Cayman Islands exchange control, including permission to open and operate dollar bank accounts in the Islands and to place dollar funds on term deposits with Cayman Island banks and trust companies.

Persons and companies from outside the sterling area carrying on business in the Islands must have their businesses designated as "resident for exchange control", but they may be authorized to remit to outside the sterling area all profits, including capital gains, free from Exchange Control restrictions.

Financial and Professional Services

Modern trust and company laws are evidence of the government's desire to encourage use of the tax-haven facilities, both for investment within the Islands and as a shelter from taxation in respect of operations elsewhere.

There is a Law Society on Grand Cayman; its members being solicitors, barristers and law agents. While the latter deal principally with domestic matters, most solicitors and barristers are experienced and competent in the handling of matters associated with tax havens. Several large firms of accountants also have offices on the islands.

Five banks of international standing provide full commercial banking facilities, including the maintenance of accounts in foreign currencies. Full corporate and trust services, including provision of registered offices, directors, officers and nominee shareholders are available through the trust companies associated with these banks.

Internal Tax Structure

There are no taxes whatsoever on income or profits, capital, or capital gains. There are no death duties, no sales taxes and no withholding taxes. Thus any person in receipt of remuneration from any source in the Islands is not liable to any Cayman tax on such income. The same applies to all capital and other such payments. The revenue of the islands is derived from a duty, at present not exceeding 20 per cent, on all imports and stamp duty on most documents. Not only do taxes on income and capital not exist at present, but, by incorporating an exempted company or an exempted trust, it is possible to obtain from the Governor a guaranteed exemption from all taxes of this nature, in the case of an exempted company for a period not extending beyond 1993, and in the case of an exempted trust for up to fifty years from the date it is created.

Tax Treaties

As there are no income or withholding taxes in the Islands there are no tax treaties, and all payments to an entity within the Islands are usually subject to the maximum rates of withholding taxes in the country in which they arise.

Available Entities

The Company

The incorporation of an ordinary company in the Cayman Islands is relatively easy. Every company requires a memorandum of association to which at least three subscribers are required, each subscriber taking at least one share. This memorandum can be in the usual form, or modified to suit particular needs, provided it includes:

(*a*) the name of the company, which must end with the word Limited or its abbreviation Ltd. (in accordance with usual practice the name must not conflict with that of any other existing Cayman company);
(*b*) the address of the registered office;
(*c*) the objects for which the company is formed;
(*d*) a statement that the shareholders have limited liability;
(*e*) the amount of the authorized capital, the number and par value of the shares. (It is normally expressed in local currency but this is not essential and may, with Exchange Control permission, be quoted in any currency.)

When a memorandum is presented to the Registrar of Companies with the appropriate fee (J.$80 is the minimum and covers an authorized capital of up to J.$160,000) he will register the company immediately and issue a certificate of incorporation. Articles of association (which require a J.$6·00 stamp) are usually filed along with the memorandum but they may be filed at any time. If no articles are filed "Table A" as set out in the Banks and Trust Companies Regulation Law 1966 will apply. "Table A" will also apply even when articles are filed to the extent that it is not specifically excluded by those articles. A company must affix its name on the outside of its office and must maintain:

(*a*) a register of members;
(*b*) a register of mortgages and charges;
(*c*) a register of directors and officers.

The annual return which must be submitted by each ordinary company in January of each year, together with a fee of J.$40, is a very simple affair and contains:

(*a*) name of the company;
(*b*) address of registered office;
(*c*) authorized capital;

(*d*) issued capital;
(*e*) names and addresses of members (no disclosure of the name of the beneficial owner is required).

No Cayman company is required to file accounts, although the law provides that records must be maintained of all receipts and payments, purchases and sales, assets and liabilities. There is no requirement as to auditors.

The cost of incorporating an ordinary company with a capital of J.$160,000 is approximately J.$400.

If full corporate services are provided a trust company may charge no initial fee and the annual fee will of course depend on the amount of work involved. For the normal holding company with only one or two directors' meetings per year, this could be J.$400 in addition to the Registrar's fee of J.$40 and any out of pocket expenses. Accounting services other than a simple statement of payments and receipts would be additional.

Most of the companies incorporated in the Cayman Islands are investment holding companies, holding quoted or unquoted investments throughout the world. Some companies are incorporated in connection with the invoicing of goods from one country to another, others are formed to own and operate ships, and others act as brokers and buy and sell in their own right on behalf of outside beneficial owners. Some may have been incorporated as subsidiaries of their parent companies in other countries for specific purposes, *e.g.* the construction, and possibly the operation, of a hotel in Hong Kong; the exploiting in Canada of copyrights, performing rights or patents; the provision of management and consultant services in connection with a housing development in South America. The scope of the use of Cayman companies is of course infinite and these are only examples.

The Exempt Company

The Cayman Islands law also permits the incorporation of exempt companies. Such a company can obtain a guarantee from the Government that no income tax, capital gains tax or capital tax, will be levied on it, and that there will be no estate or inheritance tax on its shares or debentures, for a fixed number of years but not extending beyond 1993. In addition an exempt company is exempt from several provisions of the company laws. It may, for instance, issue shares of no par value, and it need not include the word "Limited" in its name or even hold an annual meeting of shareholders. From the secrecy point of view, the company need not disclose to the Registrar the names of its shareholders. The costs of maintaining and incorporating such a company are of course higher.

The minimum incorporation fee for an exempted company is J.$750. This covers an authorized capital of up to J.$400,000. If a higher authorized capital is required the incorporation fee will be one-tenth of 1 per cent with a maximum of J.$1,600. Annual Statutory Fees are one-twentieth of 1 per cent of authorized capital with a minimum of J.$200 and a maximum of J.$1,000. Legal costs for incorporating, and costs of maintenance of an exempt company are approximately 50 per cent higher than for an ordinary company apart, of course, from the much higher registration fees. Only exempt companies may use bearer shares, and even then only when dealing with non-residents of the Scheduled Territories.

There is no stamp duty on the transfer of shares, and their par value may be expressed, with exchange control permission where necessary, in any currency. Shares may be issued at a premium, and a company may also issue redeemable preference shares which it may redeem at any time. Redeemed shares must be repaid as set out in the company's constitution and may be repaid at a premium. The funds to provide the redemption of the shares and any redemption premium must have been provided out of the profits of the company or out of the share premium account, if any. The use of non-cumulative, non-voting, redeemable preference shares (in bearer form where allowed) issued at a premium and later redeemed at a premium, is often used by clients. The share premium account can of course be capitalized in the usual way if required.

It should be noted in passing that under the banks and trust companies licensing law no company may include the words "bank" or "trust" in its name, or carry on banking or trust business, without obtaining a licence from the Governor in Council.

It is also possible to register a foreign company to carry on business in Cayman. The initial registration costs are J.$200 and the subsequent annual fee is J.$100. The foreign company must file a copy of its memorandum and articles, its address in the Islands and the name of its representative. Its country of incorporation and the fact that its shareholders' liability is limited must appear on its letterhead and advertisement.

The Trust

As with the Companies Law, the Cayman trust law is modern in concept and practice, having been enacted in 1967. There are no restrictions whatsoever on who may settle funds in a Cayman trust, although it is recommended that the prospective settlor should consider appointing as his trustee one of the reputable trust companies in the Islands. The settlor need not be physically present in Cayman, and if he wishes to sign the deed himself he can do so anywhere in the world and have his signature attested by a notary public. Alternatively, he can appoint an attorney in Cayman to sign it on his behalf or even, if he wishes, have his prospective trustee execute a declaration of trust. In any event the amount of assets stated in the deed need only be nominal, as subsequently other funds or assets may be transferred to the trust at any time. There are no statutory restrictions on income accumulation as the trustees have, by law, the right to borrow on the security of trust funds. As the common law rules against perpetuities apply it is necessary, if a considerable accumulation period is desired, to consider creating an exempt trust, which allows an accumulation period of up to one hundred years. The normal Cayman trust is usually in a discretionary settlement form. The cost of setting up such a trust would be around J.$250 including stamp duty and a normal fee for recording the deed. There are no annual Government fees for such a trust.

The Exempt Trust

The exempt trust is a concept unique to the Cayman Islands, in that the rule of accumulations does not, as already mentioned, apply. An exempt trust can obtain a 50-year guarantee exempting it from any future taxation in the Cayman Islands on both capital and income. As the law provides for all interests in expectancy, which might otherwise be deemed to vest in any beneficiary, to vest in the Registrar of Trusts no prospective beneficiary can therefore be deemed to have any taxable interest until assets are specifically transferred or appointed to him. This does not leave the beneficiary at the mercy of an unscrupulous trustee, as the Registrar of Trusts would act at once in the event of any breach of trust in order to protect the interest of any prospective beneficiary. The cost of setting up such a trust would be about J.$525, including an initial government fee of J.$200 payable on the application for registration. This application must be made prior to execution of the deed and after provisional approval the deed must be executed and filed with the Registrar within twenty-eight days of that approval. After registration, an annual fee must be paid in March of each year. This is J.$100, or if the income of the trust is smaller than J.$100, the entire income. It must however be kept in mind that no resident of the Cayman Islands may be a beneficiary of an exempt trust. If any beneficiary subsequently becomes a resident this would not void the trust but the Government's guarantee of tax exemption would not apply to such a beneficiary's interest.

GIBRALTAR

GIBRALTAR INTERNATIONAL TRUST CORPORATION LIMITED

The rock of Gibraltar, a bold mountainous promontory, stands out steeply and impressively from the adjoining low-lying Spanish territory to which it is connected by a sandy isthmus. The Spanish port of Algeciras lies five miles across the Bay to the west and Africa twenty miles across the Straits to the south. The Rock runs from north to south for a length of nearly three miles and is three-quarters of a mile wide having a total area of two and a quarter square miles.

The climate of Gibraltar is temperate. Snow or frost is extremely rare and the mean minimum and maximum temperatures during the winter months are 54°F. and 65°F. respectively. During the summer the climate is humid and relaxing and the minimum and maximum temperatures are 65°F. and 85°F. respectively.

Gibraltar was settled in 711 by Moors. Possession alternated between them and Spain for several hundred years until they were finally driven out in 1462. Spain then held the Rock until 1704 when it fell to an Anglo-Dutch fleet under Admiral Rooke during the war of the Spanish succession. Gibraltar was ceded to Britain for all time by Article 10 of the Treaty of Utrecht signed in 1713. The cession to Britain was subsequently confirmed by five other Treaties—the Treaties of Seville (1792); Vienna (1731); Aix-la-Chapelle (1756); Paris (1763) and Versailles (1783). Since the departure of the Spanish garrison in 1704, the Spanish population in Gibraltar has been small. Most of the 20,000 Gibraltarians are of Genoese or British descent whose ancestors settled in Gibraltar in the eighteenth century attracted by the opportunities for trade and prosperity offered by Gibraltar's geographical position. Today, the people of Gibraltar are a homogeneous and prosperous community, playing a full part in the conduct of their domestic affairs.

Communications

Gibraltar is linked to the outside world by both sea and air. The flying time between Gibraltar and London by Trident Jet aircraft is

2½ hours. Tangier on the north coast of Africa can be reached by sea (2½ hours) or air (20 minutes).

Although Gibraltar is joined to the Spanish mainland, there is no communication by land for pedestrian and vehicular traffic. The Gibraltar frontier on the British side remains open, but Spain has closed her land frontier to all traffic.

Commercial cable and radio services, which are operated in association with Cable & Wireless Limited, include public service telegraphy, telephone and telex.

Government

The "decolonization" of Gibraltar has been a subject which has received the attention of the United Nations over the past six or seven years following Spain's pressures to acquire the sovereignty of the territory. In September 1967, a referendum was held in Gibraltar in which the people of Gibraltar were invited to say which of the following alternative courses would best serve their interests:

(*a*) to pass under Spanish sovereignty in accordance with the terms proposed by the Spanish Government to the Government of the United Kingdom on the 18th May 1966, or

(*b*) voluntarily to retain their link with the United Kingdom with democratic local institutions and with the United Kingdom retaining its present responsibilities.

12,138 votes were cast for alternative B and only 44 for alternative A.

As a result of constitutional talks held in Gibraltar in July 1968 between representatives of the United Kingdom Government and of the Gibraltar Government and other political parties, agreement was reached on a new constitution for Gibraltar which came into operation following a general election in the Spring of 1969. Under the new Constitution the former legislative Council and the City Council or Municipal Authority were replaced by a new Body called the Gibraltar House of Assembly consisting of fifteen elected members and two ex-officio members, the Attorney General and the Financial Secretary. The Council of Ministers was retained and ministers were entrusted with full responsibility for matters of domestic concern. Responsibility for external affairs, defence and internal security remain with Her Majesty's Government.

The preamble to the Order in Council, which promulgated the new constitution, contains recitals to the effect that Gibraltar is part of Her Majesty's Dominions and will remain so unless and until an act of Parliament otherwise provides, and furthermore that Her Majesty's Government have made it clear that they will never hand over the people of Gibraltar to another State against their freely and democratically expressed wishes.

Law

The substantive Law of Gibraltar consists partly of the English statutes as contained in the Gibraltar Application of English Law Ordinance, recent acts of Parliament expressly or by necessary implication applied to the territory, the common law to date, Orders in Council relating to Gibraltar and locally enacted Ordinances and subsidiary legislation.

The Courts of Law consist of the Supreme Court, the Court of First Instance and the Magistrates' Court. In certain cases appeals lie from decisions of the Supreme Court to the Court of Appeal and thence to the Privy Council. The Judiciary is at present comprised of the Chief Justice, the Judge of the Court of First Instance, a Stipendiary Magistrate and Justices of the Peace. The Attorney General is the Law Officer of the Crown. Barristers called to the Gibraltar Bar are permitted by law to act as solicitors, and solicitors enrolled at the Supreme Court of Gibraltar are at liberty to act as barristers.

Language

Although English is the official language of the territory, most Gibraltarians are bilingual, Spanish being the second language. Teaching in schools, the work of the Administration, and Court proceedings are all conducted in English.

Currency and Exchange Control

The unit of currency is the Gibraltar pound which is on a par with the pound sterling. Decimalization was introduced in February 1971.

Gibraltar is within the Scheduled Territories and is therefore subject to exchange control regulations. There are no restrictions on the transfer of sterling funds to or from Gibraltar from or to any part of the Scheduled Territories. Companies which are considered resident for exchange control purposes and which trade with countries outside the Scheduled Territories may operate "retained dollar accounts" with the permission of the Financial and Development Secretary who is the Exchange Control Authority. Companies or firms incorporated outside Gibraltar which are non-resident for exchange control purposes are permitted to operate external accounts. Equally so, companies may be incorporated in Gibraltar by non-residents of the Scheduled Territories and, upon being designated "non-resident" by the Financial Secretary, can also operate external accounts.

Financial and Professional Services

The legal and accountancy professions are well represented. Members of all the professions practising in Gibraltar have pursued their studies and have qualified in the United Kingdom. There are now 12 lawyers practising in Gibraltar all of whom are members of the English Bar. As two branches of the legal profession are fused, all of them are entitled to practise as solicitors. There are several firms of chartered accountants which have offices in Gibraltar and in addition a number of English firms send out representatives to Gibraltar to audit the accounts of companies or firms when required. Five banks operate in Gibraltar.

Internal Tax Structure

Individuals and companies resident in Gibraltar (other than companies enjoying the exemptions mentioned later) are liable to tax on:

(*a*) income accruing in, derived from, or received in Gibraltar, and
(*b*) dividends, interest or emoluments of office wherever they may accrue, or be derived from, or be received.

Profits from a business enterprise carried on wholly outside Gibraltar do not attract tax unless such profits are remitted to Gibraltar and provided that the enterprise is not managed and controlled from Gibraltar.

Income Tax

The highest rate of Gibraltar income tax for individuals is 30p. and for the companies the standard rate is 37½p. in the £. Reduced rates apply to the first £3,500 of individuals' income.

There is no tax on capital or wealth and no capital gains tax.

Death Duties

All property both real and personal situate in Gibraltar which passes on the death of any person is liable to estate duty and, in the case of a deceased person who at the time of his death was domiciled in the territory, includes personal property wherever it may be. Estate duty is charged on a sliding scale which reaches a maximum of 20 per cent on estates exceeding £100,000.

Shares in, loans made to, or debentures held in an exempt company are exempt from estate duty, provided that no Gibraltarian or resident of Gibraltar is interested in such loans or debentures or that these are not secured upon immovable property situated in Gibraltar.

Tax on Sales: Stamp Duty

There is no sales tax as such but documents transferring assets require to be stamped: *ad valorem* stamp duty is charged on a sliding scale, which reaches a maximum of 1·25 per cent where the consideration exceeds £500. If however the property is situated out of Gibraltar, the document carries only a fixed duty of 50p. if under seal, or 3p. if under hand.

Stamp duty is also payable on certain other documents but the amounts are not significant.

Tax on Dividends and Interest

Exempt companies mentioned below are not liable to any withholding tax on dividends. Any other company resident in Gibraltar must deduct tax at the standard rate when paying dividends and annual interest. Interest yielded by bank accounts held in Gibraltar by persons not ordinarily resident and by exempt companies is not subject to Gibraltar income tax.

Non-residents

Remuneration received by non-residents from exempt companies is not liable to any form of tax.

Although Gibraltar's tax laws do not contain any specific provisions exempting certain trusts from payment of income tax in practice no tax liability arises in respect of trusts in which no beneficial interest accrues to any person ordinarily resident in Gibraltar.

Tax Treaties

Gibraltar has no tax treaties with any country. The White Paper recently published by the British Government in connection with Britain's entry into the Common Market states that Gibraltar will be covered by Article 227(4) of the Treaty of Rome which enjoins that the treaty provisions shall apply to the European territories for whose external relations a member state is responsible. But, since Gibraltar is not a part of the United Kingdom's customs territory, it has been agreed, at Gibraltar's request, that she should not be included in the customs territory of the enlarged Community.

It is not expected that the legislation creating the "exempt" company will be affected by Gibraltar's entry into the Common Market.

Available Entities

The Company

The Gibraltar Companies Ordinance is based on the English Companies Act of 1929 and makes similar provision for the incorporation of companies. The private company limited by shares is most widely used: it can be used for the holding of property, investment portfolios, royalties and patents, the performing of services and the carrying out of any form of trade or business. Companies can be speedily formed by registration of the necessary documents.

The Exempt Company

Gibraltar became firmly established as a tax haven with the passing of legislation in the shape of the Companies (Taxation & Concessions)

Ordinance, which grants income tax and estate duty concessions to companies incorporated in Gibraltar and registered as "exempt" as provided in the Ordinance. To qualify for an exemption certificate a company must comply with the following basic conditions.

(*a*) It must have a paid up share capital of at least £100.
(*b*) It must not, without specific approval, carry on any trade or business in Gibraltar, other than the buying, selling, holding, managing, rendering or promoting services, investments, property, choses in action and things situated outside Gibraltar.
(*c*) The company does not keep, and is prohibited by its memorandum or articles of association from keeping, any register of shares outside Gibraltar.
(*d*) No Gibraltarian or resident of Gibraltar shall be beneficially interested in any of its shares. Transferees of shares in an exempt company must be approved by the Financial and Development Secretary.

An exempt company can virtually engage in any type of activity or business in any part of the world which does not involve any person or company ordinarily resident in Gibraltar other than another exempt company. Although no Gibraltarians or residents of Gibraltar may hold any beneficial interest in the shares of an exempt company, they may nevertheless hold such shares as nominees or trustees.

When applying for an exemption certificate a company must furnish to the Financial and Development Secretary the names of its directors, beneficial owners of its shares, and of its auditors, the nature of its proposed activities and its share capital structure. This information is sent under confidential cover and the Companies Ordinance contains provisions as to secrecy to ensure that the identity of the beneficial shareholders so acquired is not divulged to any person or authority abroad. The only information which is public is that which appears on the Register of Companies and includes particulars of the directors and registered shareholders.

An exemption certificate grants full exemption from Gibraltar income tax and estate duty and is valid for 25 years from the date of issue, provided that the annual tax or fee is paid and that the other requirements of the legislation are complied with.

The annual tax or licence fee is a flat rate of £225 in the case of an exempt company which is ordinarily resident in Gibraltar, and £200 in the case of an exempt company which is not so ordinarily resident. The annual tax is payable in advance in two six-monthly instalments.

There are no restrictions on the appointment of directors who can be of any nationality and reside anywhere in the world. Gibraltarians can also be appointed as directors of exempt companies.

An exempt company which seeks designation as non-resident for exchange control purposes, is required to express its share capital in any currency other than sterling. Once designated as non-resident, an exempt company may issue bearer shares provided that none of its shareholders or other person interested in any share is domiciled or ordinarily resident in the United Kingdom and the certificates for such bearer shares can be retained outside the Scheduled Territories by their owners.

Formation

Companies limited by shares are incorporated under the Companies Ordinance, the provisions of which are almost identical to those of Britain's 1929 Companies Act.

The formation of a company can take from about two days to about two weeks, depending on the type of articles required, which have to be printed. If standard articles are to be used, a company can be formed within 48 hours.

The essential requirements for a private limited company are as follows:

(i) a minimum of two original subscribers;
(ii) a minimum issued capital of £100 if the company is to be an exempt company;
(iii) name to be approved by the Registrar of Companies;
(iv) registered address within Gibraltar.

A company is incorporated by filing the necessary documents at the Registry of Companies and upon payment of the registration fees.

The professional costs or fees for the formation of a company are in the region of £100. The approximate cost of forming a private limited company with a nominal share capital of £100 (which is the minimum required for an exempt company) is £150 inclusive of professional fees, duty, registration and filing fees, and the cost of the company books (register of members and minute book) and the company seal.

If the company is to be an exempt company, application has to be made to the Financial Secretary for its registration as such once it has been incorporated and shares allotted as fully paid up to a value of at least £100. No licence or consent is required for the formation of a company, the shareholders in which are all residents of the Scheduled Territories.

A company wishing to be designated as non-resident of the Scheduled Territories must obtain the permission of the Financial Secretary and must also express its share capital in a currency other than sterling.

The only requirements which have to be met by a company, are the filing of notices relating to its registered address or any changes thereof, to the allotment of its shares, and to the appointment of its directors. A return containing a list of all persons who on the fourteenth day after the first or only ordinary general meeting in the year are members of the company, and of all persons who have ceased to be members, must be filed once a year. Such annual return must also state the address of the registered office and contain particulars of the share capital of the company showing the shares allotted and the amounts called up on each share, particulars of the persons who are the directors of the company and the total amount of the indebtedness of the company in respect of all mortgages and charges required to be registered.

The annual maintenance cost for a company depends largely on the nature of the services to be performed. The annual fee or charge for providing the registered office and secretarial services to include filing of necessary notices is about £100.

If nominee facilities in the form of directors and shareholders are to be provided, the annual operating charges are usually subject to negotiation.

A private limited company which obtain an exemption certificate as an exempt company is not liable to any taxes other than the payment of the annual licence fee.

The Trust

The concept of trust known to English law is also to be found in the laws of Gibraltar. The Trustee Ordinance which is based on the English Trustee Act of 1893, lays down the powers and duties of trustees and the powers of the Court in relation to trusts.

As mentioned earlier, it is not the practice of the Gibraltar income tax authorities to tax trusts in which no beneficial interest accrues to any person ordinarily resident in Gibraltar and the income from which is not received in Gibraltar, even if the trustees of such trusts are resident in Gibraltar.

The Partnership

The term "partnership" is applied to the relation which subsists between persons carrying on a business in common with a view of profit. A partnership can be created simply by the execution of a deed by all the partners who are to participate in the partnership. There is no requirement in law for the registration of such deeds.

If a partnership has a place of business in Gibraltar and carries on business under a name which does not consist of the true surnames of all the partners, then it must be registered under the Business Names (Registration) Ordinance. This registration is effected by filing at the Registry of the Supreme Court a prescribed form containing particulars as to the name of the business, its general nature, the principal place of business, names of the partners, and the date of commencement of the business. The only fee payable is 25p.

The Limited Partnerships Ordinance provides for the formation of limited partnerships under which the liability to third parties of the partners who take no part in the management of the partnership business is limited to a specified amount. Limited partnerships must be registered in the Registry of the Supreme Court, and pay a fee of £2 upon registration.

A partnership is not treated as a distinct legal entity, but consists merely of the partners as separate legal persons carrying on business together, mutually bound to each other by the terms of the partnership agreement. The partners are taxed on their share of the partnership profits. Non-resident partners do not enjoy any special exemption from tax, such as is accorded to exempt companies and their shareholders; but if the business of the partnership is conducted outside Gibraltar the profits are not liable to tax in Gibraltar.

HONG KONG

THE CHARTERED BANK HONG KONG TRUSTEE LIMITED

Paradoxically, Hong Kong's advantages as a tax haven arise in part from the fact that it is not a tax haven in the true sense of that term. Hong Kong taxes Hong Kong source business profits and income, the present rate being 15 per cent, but its freedom of exchange, its limitation of tax to Hong Kong source profits and income and its leading place as the manufacturing and trading centre of South East Asia enable many operations to be set up which have "a legitimate business purpose" within the meaning of tax legislation elsewhere and which avoid the suspicion and adverse discriminatory treatment with which such operations in pure tax havens are often treated by the tax officials of high tax rate countries.

Geographically, Hong Kong lies on the south-east coast of China, bordering on Kwantung Province. It has a total land area of about 398 square miles of which about 33 square miles comprising Hong Kong Island, Kowloon, Stonecutters Island and a number of small islands are British territory, and of which New Kowloon and the New Territories, including the major islands of Lantao and Lamma and many smaller islands, having an area of about 365 square miles, are territory leased from China. The lease expires on the 30th June, 1997.

Communications

Hong Kong is connected by B.O.A.C. and other major airlines to Japan, the United States, Australasia, Europe, the United Kingdom and destinations en route, and there are frequent passenger and cargo services to ports in all parts of the world. Telephone, telegraph and telex services are excellent.

Government

Hong Kong has a Colonial Government, the constitution being prescribed by Letters Patent under the Great Seal of the United

Kingdom. The Government comprises the Governor, the Executive Council and the Legislative Council with an Urban Council which deals primarily with municipal matters. The Executive Council consists of five ex-officio and one nominated official members and eight unofficial members also nominated by the Governor. The eight unofficial members at present include four Chinese members. There are no elected members. The Legislative Council comprises the Governor (who is President of the Council and has a casting vote), four ex-officio members and eight nominated civil servants making a total on the official side of thirteen and thirteen unofficial members nominated by the Governor. Eleven of the thirteen unofficial members are at present Chinese but again there are no elected members.

The principal function of the Executive Council is to advise the Governor on matters of importance affecting the Colony but the final responsibility for taking and implementing decisions lies with the Governor. Should the Governor act contrary to the advice given by the majority of members of the Executive Council, he must report his reasons to the Secretary of State for the Colonies in England. The Governor in Council further has extensive powers of passing subsidiary legislation in the form of rules, regulations and orders and also hears appeals and petitions under a number of Ordinances.

The Legislative Council, as its name suggests, is the law making body, the laws of the Colony being enacted by the Governor with the advice and consent of the Legislative Council. It also controls public expenditure through its Finance Committee.

Law

Under the provisions of the Application of English Law Ordinance, the common law and rules of equity in England are in force in Hong Kong so far as they may be applicable to the circumstances of Hong Kong or its inhabitants and subject to such modification thereto as circumstances may require, save to the extent that such common law or rules of equity may from time to time be modified or excluded by any Order in Council which applies to Hong Kong, or any Act of Parliament which applies to Hong Kong or any Ordinance. The Supreme Court Ordinance provides that subject to the provisions thereof, the practice of the Supreme Court of Judicature of England for the time being in force shall be in force in the Supreme Court of Hong Kong.

Language

Although the vast majority of the population is Chinese, speaking Cantonese dialect, English is the language used for virtually all business and commerce except when only Chinese persons are involved. Government is currently studying four reports on the use of Cantonese as an "official" language and has given approval in principle to the institution of simultaneous translation in the Legislative and Urban Councils to implement one of the recommendations in the first report. Government is also making an increasing effort to conduct correspondence between those Departments which deal primarily in Chinese matters, and the Chinese community, in Chinese but this is a formidable task because written Chinese, being composed from characters instead of an alphabet, and having no tenses in the Western sense, does not readily adapt to present day requirements for official and commercial communications and cannot be reproduced on normal typewriters or office machines.

Currency and Exchange Control

The currency is the Hong Kong dollar.

Hong Kong is unique as a major financing centre in being a member of the sterling area but, at the same time, having a free exchange market in which sterling area currencies can be freely exchanged for United States Dollars and other non-sterling area currencies.

Prior to April 1967, exchange control was governed by the Defence (Finance) Regulations based on the war-time legislation in England but these regulations were not enforced by Government and the free exchange market operated with Government's tacit approval. Such transactions, were, however, technically illegal and could not be enforced through the Courts. In April 1967, the position was regularized by the passing of the Defence (Finance) Regulations (Validation of Contracts) Ordinance, No. 29 of 1967 and the Proclamation of a general consent by the Governor under the existing Regulations in respect of all lawful transactions arising in the ordinary course of business in which one of the persons involved is resident or carries on trade or business in Hong Kong. The combined effect of the new Ordinance and the Proclamation is that, provided a transaction is otherwise lawful, and provided it is in the ordinary course of business, and one of the parties resides or carries on business in Hong Kong, the free exchange market can legally be used, and contractual and other obligations arising therefrom can be enforced in the Hong Kong Courts.

It should be emphasized however that exchange control is still exercised in Hong Kong to prevent sterling, and other sterling area currencies, from being remitted into Hong Kong by non-residents and then converted through the free exchange market into non-sterling area currencies. The market is intended for the use and benefit of those who reside or carry on business in Hong Kong, and its abuse by residents of other places in the sterling area to evade their own exchange control regulations could well lead to restriction of its present freedom.

Financial and Professional Services

Hong Kong's professional, commercial and financial facilities are unequalled in South East Asia and compare favourably with most parts of the world.

Legal and accountancy services are readily available with a considerable degree of expertise in nominee and off-shore operations. A number of the leading world-wide accountancy firms have offices or correspondents in Hong Kong; many of the leading brokerage houses have established offices or representative offices; investment advice is obtainable through specialist advisers, brokerage houses and banks, and there is a large volume of investment in the United States, Canadian, British and, to a lesser extent, Australian markets. There is no dollar premium for United States investments, but currency for non-sterling area investments has to be purchased through the free market at prevailing rates.

Banking services are excellent and diverse. As at 31st December, 1971, there was a total of 73 banks registered under the Banking Ordinance including, in addition to those established in Hong Kong, banks from the United States, England, France, Germany, Belgium, Holland, China, India, Indonesia, Malaysia, Singapore and elsewhere. In addition 37 overseas banks had, at that date, established representative offices for liaison with customers wishing to hold accounts with, or make investments through, their home offices.

Hong Kong is the leading port of South East Asia and both shipping and airline services are frequent and offer direct connections to most parts of the world. Postal, telex and telegraphic services are speedy and efficient and although there is still a shortage of telephones in some areas due to a world record rate of expansion, the local Telephone Company is making rapid progress in clearing the back-log.

Internal Tax Structure

Income and Profits

Taxes on income and profits are collected under four heads, namely:

(1) property tax;
(2) salaries tax;
(3) profits tax;
(4) interest tax;

but all apply only to Hong Kong source income or profits and all are at present subject to an overriding maximum of 15 per cent.

Property tax is charged at the standard rate of 15 per cent on the rateable value of land and buildings situate within the Colony with an exemption for owner occupied property and an allowance for repairs and maintenance.

Salaries tax is charged on all remuneration from any employment, office, pension or similar income arising in or derived from Hong Kong. The tax is charged at graduated percentages of the standard rate of 15 per cent. After allowances, the rate commences at $2\frac{3}{4}$ per cent on the first H.K.$5,000 and rises at H.K.$5,000 intervals to a maximum of 30 per cent but with an overall limitation to 15 per cent of the gross amount before allowances.

Remuneration for services performed wholly outside Hong Kong and other income of a similar nature not arising in or derived from Hong Kong is not taxable.

Profits tax is charged at the standard rate of 15 per cent on the net profits after depreciation allowances of every individual, partnership or corporation carrying on business in the Colony. The tax is assessed on a preceding year basis.

Interest tax is charged at the standard rate of 15 per cent on interest in excess of $3\frac{1}{2}$ per cent per annum arising in or derived from the

Colony and the tax is generally deducted at source by the payer except where payment is made to a corporation which is itself subject to profits tax.

Capital or Wealth

Hong Kong does not tax capital or wealth.

Capital Gains

There is no capital gains tax and no tax on gifts.

Death Duties

Death duties are charged in the form of estate duty but only on property situated in Hong Kong. The legislation is based on the English legislation but in much simpler form and where a controlled company falls to be valued on an assets basis, duty is only chargeable on the proportion of its assets which are in Hong Kong.

Rates run from 5 per cent on estates over H.K.$200,000 (approx. £13,750 sterling) and less than H.K.$300,000 (approx. £20,625 sterling) to a maximum of 15 per cent on estates in excess of H.K.$2,000,000 (approx. £137,500 sterling).

Sales Taxes

There are no sales taxes as such but duties are imposed under the Dutiable Commodities Ordinance on certain items such as liquors, tobacco, hydrocarbon oils, table waters and methyl alcohol if manufactured in or imported into the Colony.

Imports and Exports

Although these are not taxed, regulations were passed in 1966 for the purpose of raising revenue for trade promotion under which a declaration has to be filed with the Department of Commerce and Industry in respect of all goods imported into or exported from the Colony on which a minimum fee of H.K.$2·00 is charged on the value of goods up to H.K.$4,000 and thereafter at the rate of H.K.$0·50 for each additional H.K.$1,000 of the value.

Stamp Duties

Stamp duties are charged on documents under the Stamp Ordinance which is similar to the corresponding English legislation. Charges which are likely to affect transactions within the scope of this publication are the charge of H.K.$0·40 per H.K.$100 on the consideration paid on the transfer of shares on a register maintained in the Colony, the charge of H.K.$0·25 per H.K.$1,000 on bills of exchange and promissory notes (including unsecured loan notes issued by a company) drawn, issued or negotiated in the Colony and on all foreign exchange transactions and the charge of H.K.$2·00 per H.K.$1,000 on mortgages and debentures.

Dividends and Withholding Taxes

Dividends are not taxed in Hong Kong whether received from a Hong Kong company or an overseas company. The Inland Revenue Ordinance exempts from tax any dividend received from a corporation which is itself subject to profits tax; and dividends from overseas corporations are necessarily non-Hong Kong source income. This applies whether the recipient is resident or non-resident.

Tax Treaties

As Hong Kong does not tax non-Hong Kong source income, it has not entered into any tax treaties or conventions with other countries. There is some relief against double taxation under the Inland Revenue Ordinance in respect of income already taxed in another British Commonwealth territory only, and taxes paid in Hong Kong are eligible for the foreign tax credit against United States taxes under the United States Internal Revenue Code.

Available Entities

Hong Kong law generally follows the pattern of English law although in commercial matters it is often less restrictive and frequently less up to date. Company law, a revision of which is at present under con-consideration by a revision Committee, is based on the English Companies Act 1929 with some of the 1948 Act amendments. The Partnership Ordinance follows the lines of the English Partnership Act 1890 and trusts are partly governed by the Trustee Ordinance which is similar to the English Trustee Act 1925.

There are the same rules as in England regarding the indefinite postponement of vesting of trust interests and the periods for which accumulation of income can be directed. The perpetuities and Accumulations Ordinance No. 26 of 1970 permits accumulations for any of six periods:

(1) the life of the grantor or settlor;
(2) 21 years from the death of the grantor, settlor or testator;
(3) the minority of any person in being at the death of the grantor, testator or settlor;
(4) the minority of any person who would if of full age be entitled under the instrument directing the accumulation to the income directed to be accumulated;
(5) 21 years from the date of the making of the disposition;
(6) the minority of any person in being at the date of making the disposition.

If longer periods are required, these can be achieved by empowering trustees to incorporate one or more limited companies which do not declare dividends unless and until a distribution of income is required. The absence of any tax on dividends or any deemed distribution provisions avoids any tax disadvantages of this procedure so far as Hong Kong is concerned.

The entities most likely to be of use in tax planning matters are the Hong Kong incorporated company, the foreign company with a branch registered in Hong Kong and the Hong Kong trust, each of which is considered below.

The Company

No prior permission or clearance from exchange control or other authorities is required for the formation of a Hong Kong company, irrespective of the nationality or residence of the incorporators, unless the company intends to carry on banking or insurance business in which event the requirements of the specific Ordinances governing these activities must be complied with.

Companies are either private companies in which the number of members is limited to 50, the shares may not be offered to the public and the right to transfer shares is restricted (usually by being made subject to the approval of the directors or subject to rights of pre-emption in favour of the other shareholders), or public companies whose shares can be offered to the public and are freely transferable. Public companies are subject to control in respect of such matters as the minimum capital which must be subscribed before commencing business, the issue of prospectuses and offers for sale, and the filing of balance sheets. Private companies are not subject to these requirements and do not have to file balance sheets which are open to public inspection although they are required to submit audited balance sheets to their shareholders at each annual general meeting and to file them with the Inland Revenue Department.

Incorporation is effected by filing with the Registrar of Companies a printed form of memorandum and articles of association which, in the case of a private company must be subscribed by at least two persons for one share each, and in the case of a public company by at least seven persons, together with other supporting documents. Subscribers and ultimate shareholders can be nominees and there is no obligation to disclose the identity of beneficial owners.

Incorporation usually takes from two to four weeks and the cost of incorporation is usually in the region of H.K.$1,750 to H.K.$2,500 (approx. £120 to £170), including legal charges, registration fees, printing charges and the provision of the statutory books and seal, plus the capital duty of H.K.$2 per H.K.$1,000 on the amount of the authorized capital which is payable when the incorporation documents are filed.

Directors and shareholders may be of any nationality and place of residence. There is no requirement for any Hong Kong resident participation but the company must have a registered office in Hong Kong and if there is no resident director or officer must appoint a resident who is responsible for complying with the requirements of the Inland Revenue Ordinance, but who is not thereby rendered personally liable for payment of any tax payable by the company. Many legal, accountancy and other firms provide registered office services at fees varying from H.K.$500 per annum upwards according to the type of company and the amount of work involved.

The authorized capital can be expressed in any currency although it is usually more convenient to express it in Hong Kong dollars. In the case of a private company, there is no minimum or maximum capital requirement nor any compulsory relationship between equity and loan financing. The theoretical minimum capital is two shares of one cent each.

Where a company is being set up for purposes which may be of benefit to Hong Kong's economy and capital is being remitted into Hong Kong from overseas, application can be made to the Exchange Control Authorities for permission to remit the funds to Hong Kong at the official rate of exchange which permission will usually carry with it the right to repatriate dividends and, subject to such conditions as may be imposed, also the right to repatriate capital at the official rate of exchange. This gives a measure of protection against fluctuations in the free market rate of exchange but not, of course, against devaluation which affects the official rate itself. If it is not desired to take advantage of this procedure, capital and dividends can be remitted in and out through the free market without any application for consent, but capital invested in the form of shares other than redeemable preference shares can only be repaid by a company to its shareholders on liquidation or with the leave of the Court. This applies whether or not the capital was contributed from abroad and is wholly unconnected with exchange control legislation.

Exchange control permission is not required for the issue of the shares to persons resident outside the sterling area nor for the formation of subsidiary companies outside the sterling area.

A Hong Kong incorporated company must hold an annual meeting of its shareholders and must file an annual return with the Registrar of Companies giving particulars of its capital, shareholders, mortgages and charges, transfers of shares during the year and directors. If it carries on business within the Colony, the company must also take out an annual business registration certificate, the annual fee for which is H.K.$25. Meetings of both directors and shareholders may be held in any part of the world and even the annual meeting need not be held in Hong Kong.

The operation of a Hong Kong private limited company is both straightforward and flexible. Unless engaged in specialized business such as banking or insurance, it needs no licence or consent to commence business and can operate in any part of the world. It is only taxable in Hong Kong on its profits arising in or derived from Hong Kong and can accumulate or distribute profits without affecting its tax position. It is the ideal vehicle for business and investment operations in South East Asia and elsewhere.

For the United States citizen or corporation seeking to invest or operate in the Far East, the Hong Kong limited company offers many advantages, particularly if he can find a trustworthy non-United States partner to participate with him on an equal basis. The United States Internal Revenue Code is particularly severe in its application to foreign corporations controlled by United States citizens and, for example, assesses the United States shareholders to tax on many classes of income whether distributed or not and imposes income tax rates instead of capital gains tax rates on the proceeds of sale or liquidation of such a corporation to the extent that the proceeds represent profits accumulated since 1962. By investing through a limited company on an equal basis with a non-United States citizen, a United States investor can accumulate profits which do not fall within the definition "personal holding company income" under the Code free of tax and take the accumulations as a capital gain when he finally sells out or when the Company is liquidated.

Registered Branch of a Foreign Company

The companies Ordinance provides also for registration of branches of foreign corporations. Registration is effected by filing a certified copy of the constitution or other incorporation document, particulars of the directors and particulars of at least one person resident in Hong Kong who is authorized to accept service of process on the company's behalf. So far as Hong Kong is concerned, the tax position of the branch of a foreign corporation is identical to that of a Hong Kong incorporated company. It pays the same annual business registration fee of H.K.$25 and is taxed only on its profits arising in or derived from Hong Kong. The advantages of operating through a Hong Kong incorporated company as against a branch usually stem from the tax legislation of the country of the parent or owners and the only disadvantage of the branch from the Hong Kong viewpoint is that it is obligated to file annually with the Registrar a signed copy of its parent company's accounts which thus become available for public inspection.

The Trust

The Hong Kong trust with Hong Kong resident trustees offers many advantages to the prospective settlor. Expert trustee services are readily available, and not unduly expensive. Typical fees are an acceptance fee ranging from 2½ per cent on the first H.K.$150,000 down to three-quarters on the excess over H.K.$1,000,000. If the trust assets are invested abroad, no Hong Kong tax is payable either on capital or dividends, and the opportunities of investing anywhere in the world through the free exchange market generally outweigh the disadvantage of suffering maximum foreign withholding taxes due to the absence of double taxation treaties.

Discretionary trusts are frequently established for overseas beneficiaries, and as mentioned earlier, the problem of accumulations is usually resolved by the incorporation of one or more holding companies which do not distribute their profits to the trustees unless and until required.

Stamp duty is chargeable on settlements at the rate of H.K.$0·30 per H.K.$100 of the amount or value of the settled property within the Colony but where the settlement operates as a voluntary disposition the rate is H.K.$2 per H.K.$100. It should be noted that the duty is charged only on the value of the property within Hong Kong so that there is no charge if money or investments situated abroad are transferred to the trustees.

Investors who are concerned at the political risks can be protected by the formation of holding companies in places such as Panama and other non-sterling area tax havens and also by the inclusion of emergency provisions in trust deeds providing for changes in the trustees and in the forum of administration, either automatically or by the bringing into force of escrow documents deposited in a "safer" territory, in the event of serious political changes taking place.

The Partnership

The general law of partnership in Hong Kong is governed by the Partnership Ordinance which is based on the English Partnership Act of 1890. There is also a limited Partnership Ordinance providing for the establishment of partnerships in which one or more of the partners limits his liability but takes no part in management, and in which at least one partner, known as the General Partner, has unlimited liability; and a Chinese Partnership Ordinance containing special provisions regarding Chinese partnerships which register thereunder including a degree of limitation of liability for the partners.

Partnerships in Hong Kong are taxed as separate entities at the standard rate of 15 per cent on their business profits arising in, or derived from, the Colony, but any member thereof can elect to be personally assessed. If he does so elect, he is entitled to claim personal and other allowances against his total assessable income, and pays tax on the progressive salaries tax scale from 2¾ per cent to 30 per cent subject to the overall maximum of 15 per cent of the gross. In practice, it ceases to be worthwhile claiming personal assessment when the total income reaches between about H.K.$70,000 and H.K.$80,000 because above this amount, the portion taxed in excess of the standard rate of 15 per cent outweighs the benefit of the allowances.

Losses sustained by a partner in a partnership venture cannot be set off for tax purposes against that partner's profits from other operations.

THE ISLE OF MAN

INTERNATIONAL FINANCE & TRUST CORPORATION LIMITED

The Isle of Man lies in the Irish sea between Great Britain and Ireland. The Island is approximately 30 miles long by 10 miles wide with a total area of 227 square miles. The population is approximately 50,000 most of which is located in the two principal towns of Douglas, the capital, and Ramsey. The main business activities of the Island are agriculture and tourism together with light industry which has been attracted by the deliberate Government policy of low taxation. The climate is temperate with no extremes of temperature in either winter or summer.

COMMUNICATIONS

The Island is well served by a number of daily air and sea services from various places in the British Isles including London, Liverpool, Manchester, Blackpool, Belfast and Dublin. Sea services are provided by the Isle of Man Steam Packet Co. Ltd. which owns several sizeable boats including two drive on and drive off car ferries. The principal air services are provided by Cambrian Airways, a B.E.A. subsidiary, and British United Airways.

The business centre of the Island is located in Douglas which is well served by buses and taxis from the airport. Boat services terminate at the harbour in Douglas. Travel around the Island is best undertaken by car and a number of reputable car hire firms operate from the airport and the larger towns.

GOVERNMENT

The Isle of Man is a self governing territory forming part of the British Isles and its head is the reigning British monarch in his or her capacity as Lord of Man. The monarch is represented on the Island by a Lieutenant-Governor who is appointed by the British Home Office after consultation with the Island government.

The Isle of Man is not part of the United Kingdom of Great Britain and Northern Ireland and issues its own banknotes and internationally recognized British Passports in similar fashion to British islands and colonies in other parts of the world.

The Island has its own parliament known as the Court of Tynwald which stems from the original "Althing" founded by the Norse rulers of the Island in about 930 A.D. The Island consequently has its own systems of law and taxation and is virtually autonomous in all matters except foreign affairs and defence.

The Court of Tynwald consists of two houses known as the Keys and the Legislative Council. The House of Keys, which is the lower house, consists of 24 members elected by universal adult suffrage. The Legislative Council, or upper house, consists of the Bishop of Man, the First Deemster (Judge), the Attorney General, two persons nominated by the Lieutenant-Governor and five persons elected by the Keys who are not also members of the House of Keys. The Lieutenant-Governor presides over meetings of the whole Court of Tynwald and over the Legislative Council. A speaker is elected by the Keys to preside over its own meetings. A full discussion of the mechanics of government in the Isle of Man is beyond the scope of this work but further information with regard thereto may be found in a number of government publications.

The form of government in the Isle of Man has evolved over a period of a thousand years and there is a complete political stability within the Island. The House of Keys is, as mentioned above, a freely elected body and the great majority of its members is independent of all political parties. Party politics as such are virtually unknown in the Isle of Man.

Legislation of the United Kingdom parliament does not extend to the Isle of Man unless provision is made in the legislation to this effect and United Kingdom legislation of a purely domestic nature is not in practice extended to the Island without prior consultation with the Island government.

Law

The Island's legal system is based on common law which is analogous to English common law in most matters concerning business and commerce. Domestic statute law is enacted by Tynwald and supplemented, where applicable, by regulations made under specific statutes.

Language

The language of the Island is English and business documentation follows normal Anglo-Saxon usage. The concept of trusts is fully recognized.

Currency and Exchange Control

The exchange control position of the Isle of Man is of particular interest in that the Island is treated as one with the United Kingdom for this purpose. This can operate to considerable advantage in relation to persons or entities resident in the United Kingdom as there is no need to obtain consents for transfers to the Isle of Man.

Financial and Professional Services

The Island is well served by chartered accountants and the legal profession. Legal work is undertaken by advocates who perform the functions of both barrister and solicitor. Stockbroking facilities are readily available and all well-known types of British and foreign securities can be bought or sold. All the leading British clearing banks have branches in the Isle of Man and special mention should be made of the fact that the Isle of Man Bank Limited is a wholly owned subsidiary of the National Westminster Bank Limited. World-wide banking facilities are thus readily available.

Internal Tax Structure

The main sources of government revenue are:

(1) customs and excise duties (including purchase tax);
(2) income tax (limited to 21·25 per cent).

There are, on the other hand, no taxes under the following heads in the Isle of Man:

(1) capital or wealth taxes;
(2) capital gains taxes;
(3) death or estate duties;
(4) document taxes (stamp duties);
(5) gift taxes;
(6) corporation taxes (other than standard rate income tax);
(7) payroll taxes.

Customs and excise duties provide by far the greater portion of the Island's tax revenues.

The Island has an agreement with the United Kingdom known as the "Common Purse" whereby it undertakes to charge substantially the same customs and excise duties (including purchase tax) as the United Kingdom. The pooled revenues of the Island and the United Kingdom are then divided between the two territories according to a formula based on the respective resident populations and the number of visitors to the Island. As a result there are no customs or tariff barriers between the Island and the United Kingdom. However this arrangement may be brought to an end by either Government, subject to three months' notice. A recent Isle of Man Government Commission of enquiry has examined the Common Purse arrangement and has recommended that the agreement should remain in force.

At the time of writing it appears that the Isle of Man will become a member of the European Economic Community at the same time as the United Kingdom. The Isle of Man will therefore become a member of the enlarged Common Market tariff area which should, in due course, lead to the duty free movement of goods between the Isle of Man and the other Common Market countries including the United Kingdom. It is however possible that some modification to the above mentioned Common Purse agreement may be required (*a*) if there should be any change in the existing arrangements with regard to purchase tax in the Isle of Man or the United Kingdom or (*b*) as regards value added tax. There is at present no indication whether or not value added tax will be introduced in the Isle of Man but it has been agreed that none of the provisions of the Treaty of Rome relating to taxation need apply to the Isle of Man unless the Isle of Man so wishes. The Isle of Man will therefore be able to continue its present policy of low direct taxation.

The Standard Rate of Income Tax in the Isle of Man is at the low rate of 21·25 per cent and this tax is levied on the world income of Isle of Man resident Associations and individuals and on the Isle of

Man income of non-residents. The term "Association" includes companies and trusts. Associations are deemed tax resident in the Isle of Man by the Manx authorities if central control and management is exercised there.

There is no surtax.

The following general income tax points are of interest:

(*a*) Isle of Man resident companies are not subject to Isle of Man tax on that part of their income which is distributed to shareholders *i.e.* dividends are treated as a tax deductible expense. Amounts distributed to shareholders are, however, liable to Isle of Man income tax in the hands of the shareholder. Shareholders who are taxed on such distributions are not entitled to relief for any foreign tax paid by the company and for this reason it is not usual for Isle of Man companies receiving foreign income to distribute same by way of dividend.

(*b*) No Isle of Man income tax is payable by Isle of Man companies on income arising outside the Isle of Man when directorial control is exercised in another country. It is therefore sometimes advantageous to incorporate a company in the Isle of Man but to arrange for the control and management of such a company to be exercised from another tax haven country.

(*c*) Arrangements for the relief of double taxation exist in the Isle of Man whereby foreign tax borne by deduction or assessment is allowed as a credit against assessments made on Isle of Man residents in respect of the same income. This relief is, of course, restricted to the lesser of the Isle of Man or the foreign effective rate of tax on such income. Special arrangements exist between the Isle of Man and the United Kingdom under the Island's only double taxation convention whereby the Isle of Man tax on United Kingdom dividends and debenture interest is relieved by an equivalent repayment of United Kingdom income tax by the United Kingdom authorities.

The effect of the arrangements for the relief of foreign taxes is that a resident association or individual will not be required to pay Isle of Man income tax where income from a specific foreign country has already been taxed at a rate in excess of 21·25 per cent; the reader will appreciate that many countries impose withholding taxes in excess of this rate where income is paid to non-residents of those countries.

A system of tax deduction at source is required to be operated by Isle of Man associations and by tenants or occupiers of Isle of Man property in respect of payments of income to non-residents upon receipt of notice from the Assessor of income tax. Such notices are normally issued automatically to all associations and give rise to the need for returns of such income. Isle of Man resident agents may also be assessed to income tax in respect of the Manx income accruing to or from or collected by the agency (whether or not they are in receipt of such income) for the benefit of non-residents: in practice, therefore, such agents would normally deduct Manx income tax before making payments of income tax to non-residents. All deductions of income tax at source are made at the rate of 21·25 per cent but there is provision for repayment of income tax where the deductions at source exceed the true liability.

Bank interest is credited by Isle of Man banks to both residents and non-residents without deduction of income tax. Assessments to Manx tax of Isle of Man bank interest paid to non-residents are not normally made despite a theoretical liability and the position is analogous to that in the United Kingdom.

Non-residents who are remunerated by Isle of Man residents or resident associations for services performed in the Isle of Man are liable to Isle of Man income tax on such remuneration. Such tax would normally be deducted at source under the above mentioned provisions.

There is no system of deduction of income tax from payments to residents of the Isle of Man including companies so resident. Payments of income to non-residents are subjected to deduction of tax at source in order to minimize loss due to difficulties in collection but such deductions may, in some cases, be of no consequence to the recipient if they are relieved by double tax relief provisions in the country to which the income flows.

An Act of Tynwald known as the General Development Act 1964 came into operation on 8th December, 1964 empowering the Governor of the Isle of Man to cause the Treasurer of the Isle of Man to enter into agreements on behalf of the Government with persons (operators) wishing to carry out development in the Isle of Man where such development is likely to be of material benefit to the economy of the Isle of Man. Such agreements are, however, subject to the prior approval of both branches of Tynwald (*i.e.* The House of Keys and the Legislative Council).

The agreements may include "such undertakings on the part of the Government for the benefit of the operators as the Governor may deem necessary or desirable for the successful establishment of the proposed development". Undertakings may be included to provide, *inter alia*, for the following:

(*a*) the reduction, remission or non-imposition of income tax, rates, duties, and all or any other Government or local Government charges, fees or imposts;
(*b*) the acquisition of any land which may be necessary for the proposed development and for the leasing or vesting thereof to or in the operators either for value or for nominal rents or considerations.

An Agreement under the Act granting concessions as to taxes and over certain land has been entered into with an American owned oil company which is to establish an oil refinery in the Isle of Man.
The Act also includes certain other provisions such as a form of control over the erection or conversion of industrial premises; the details of these provisions are beyond the scope of this work. The Act was originally expressed to be valid for one year unless Tynwald should otherwise resolve and Tynewald resolved, on 20th October, 1965, to extend the Act until otherwise resolved.

Tax Treaties

Reference has been made above to the Isle of Man's only tax treaty which is with the United Kingdom and to the position thereunder with regard to dividends and debenture interest received by Isle of Man residents from the United Kingdom. The treaty has no other unusual features and its purport may best be summarized by the following extracts from the explanatory note to the United Kingdom edition of the treaty:

"Under the Arrangement . . . certain classes of income derived from one country by a resident of the other country are (subject to certain conditions) exempt from tax in the former country; these classes are shipping and air transport profits, certain trading profits not arising through a 'permanent establishment' and earnings of temporary business visitors. Government salaries and pensions are normally taxed by the paying Government only.

"Dividends and debenture interest payable by companies are not affected by the Arrangement. The system of unilateral relief . . . will continue to apply to them. In other cases where income continues to be taxable in both countries, credit is to be given by the country of the taxpayer's residence for the tax payable in the country of origin of the income.

"Provision is included for the exchange of information between the taxation authorities of the two countries."

Available Entities

All the usual Anglo-Saxon forms of business entity are recognized in the Isle of Man and include the following:

sole traderships;
friendly societies;
companies;
trusts;
unit trusts;
partnerships;
limited partnerships.

Consents may be required under the Exchange Control Act 1947 by non-resident persons or foreign persons wishing to participate in business activities based in the Isle of Man. No permission is normally required in relation to British persons resident for exchange control purposes in the sterling area but the position of other persons would require examination to ensure the exchange control requirements were met.

There are no restrictions under other laws on the business activities in the Isle of Man of non-resident persons of any nationality.

The position of residents of the Isle of Man who are not British and Manx by birth or residential qualifications may require special consideration under the aliens and commonwealth immigration laws of the United Kingdom or of the Isle of Man but a full discourse on this aspect is beyond the scope of this work. With some minor exceptions, related to the sale of goods to the public and to certain seasonal employments, United Kingdom citizens are accorded the same status in the Isle of Man as Manx individuals who are themselves technically United Kingdom Citizens.

Sole Traderships

Sole traderships call for little comment in the context of this work and their general nature will, it is assumed, be well known to the reader. They involve no formation formalities but confer no protection or status upon an individual. If conducted under a name other than that of the proprietor, full details of the proprietorship are required to be registered at the General Registry under the Registration of Business Names Acts 1918–1954. The General Registry is open to the public.

Friendly Societies

Friendly Societies exist and operate in the Isle of Man under United Kingdom legislation which was extended to the Isle of Man many years ago.

The Company

Companies are incorporated in the Isle of Man by the process of registering a memorandum and articles of association subscribed by at least two persons (seven in a case of a public company). Registration can proceed on any normal working day without delay and the time taken to form a company is limited to the time required for the drafting and printing of the memorandum and articles of association. Professional firms can usually make arrangements for incorporation to take place in seven to ten days from receipt of instructions.

Companies can have unlimited liability if desired or their liability can be limited by guarantee or by reference to their share capital. The cost of formation of a limited company with an authorized capital of, say, £2,000 is of the order of £100/£150 including all printing costs, statutory books, seal and professional fees. The cost of formation may, of course, be greater if substantial work is required in relation to setting up the company or in cases requiring a larger authorized share capital. A registration fee of between £3 and £100 is payable on incorporation of a company together with capital duty at the rate of £10 on the first £2,000 share capital and 0·36 per cent on share capital in excess of £2,000.

A Register of Companies is maintained at the General Registry which gives details of the shareholders and directors of each company together with details of charges against a company and copies of certain resolutions which require to be filed. In the case of a public company (which differs from a private company in that its shares are freely transferable without the consent of the directors) accounts are also required to be filed. There is no requirement for the filing of accounts of private companies. The annual maintenance cost of a company in the Isle of Man is dependent on the nature and extent of the duties of the directors and staff but a minimum of £150 per annum may be considered typical.

The Trust

Trusts may be formed in the Isle of Man with the minimum of formality and there are no registration requirements for *inter vivos* trusts. A trust deed is not essential but would normally be prepared. A particular advantage of the Isle of Man in relation to trusts is that there is no stamp duty and, consequently, there are no imposts on trust deeds. Trusts may be legally created in the Isle of Man by a non-resident settlor for beneficiaries resident outside the Isle of Man. In fact the Isle of Man is an ideal base for such trusts as there is no Isle of Man income tax liability on foreign trust income in such cases provided that the income is actually distributed to the non-resident beneficiaries. Even if not distributed, any Isle of Man income tax liability on foreign income may well be discharged by double tax relief in respect of foreign tax. Such trusts are, of course, liable to Isle of Man income tax at 21·25 per cent on Isle of Man income, but this may not be of material consequence if the beneficiaries live in countries which charge higher rates of tax and which grant relief from double taxation.

A suitably empowered company can act as a trustee in the Isle of Man and it is feasible to form a limited liability company to act as trustee of a specific trust thus providing perpetuity of trusteeship and other advantages.

Unit Trusts

Unit Trusts are specially catered for in the Isle of Man under the Prevention of Fraud (Investments) Act 1968 the requirements of which are, generally speaking, similar to the equivalent United Kingdom requirements. It is a specific requirement that a company desiring to act as trustee of a unit trust must have an authorized capital of £500,000 of which at least one-half must be and remain fully paid or that the company must be at least 80 per cent owned by a company which qualifies as a trustee company.

The Partnership

Partnerships may be readily formed in the Isle of Man by mutual agreement amongst the proposed partners. A partnership deed is not necessary but may often be desirable. Partnerships are regulated by the Partnership Act 1909 which contains, *inter alia,* certain provisions applicable to the relationship between partners unless the partners agree otherwise. Partnerships may be formed instantly if no partnership deed is required and formation costs are negligible. Statutory requirements are limited to (*a*) the need to register the name of the partnership under the Registration of Business Names Acts 1918–1954 if the partnership trades in the Isle of Man under a name other than that of the names of the individual partners and (*b*) the requirement to make annual income tax returns. Partnership income is assessable to tax *pro rata* on the individual partners and not on the partnership as such but recovery of income tax can in certain cases be effected from a partner acting as agent for another partner, *e.g.* from a resident partner in partnership with a non-resident.

Limited Partnerships

Limited partnerships on the English pattern, involving one or more general (unlimited) partners and one or more limited liability partners with no executive powers, are also envisaged by the Partnership Act 1909 but are not much used in practice because of the ease with which limited companies can be formed. The registration and income tax requirements of limited partnerships are similar to those for ordinary partnerships.

JERSEY

JERSEY INTERNATIONAL BANK OF COMMERCE LTD.

Jersey, the largest of the Channel Islands, lies in the English Channel, about 14 miles west of the Cherbourg Peninsula, and some 30 miles north of St. Malo, France. London is approximately 220 miles to the north-west. The island extends for approximately 10 miles from east to west and 6 miles from north to south. The total resident population is presently estimated to be in excess of 65,000 of whom some 30,000 live in the capital St. Helier, the port and principal trading area of the Island.

As evidenced by the success of the Island's tourist industry, the Island has a pleasant climate, the summer being warm and the winter mild. As it lies within the Temperate Zone, climatic extremes do not occur.

The entry of the United Kingdom into the E.E.C. will in no way detract from Jersey's standing as an international finance centre. While technically included within the Treaty of Rome, the arrangements offered to Jersey by the E.E.C. (which have been accepted by the Island's Parliament) take full account of Jersey's unique position. Under the agreed arrangements only those aspects of the Treaty concerned with free trade will apply to the Island and the exclusion from all other provisions, and particularly any element of the E.E.C.'s policy towards tax harmonization, is permanent.

Jersey will remain a secure, politically stable, and responsible finance centre of advantage to those individuals and companies seeking to minimize their international tax liabilities. Indeed, if the relaxation of the sterling exchange control restrictions, which the United Kingdom has proposed should take place between the United Kingdom and other E.E.C. countries by 1977, becomes a reality, the Island's reputation as an international finance centre is likely to be enhanced rather than diminished in the future.

Communications

The Island maintains a busy commercial harbour at St. Helier, and passenger and freight services operate to and from the United Kingdom, the other Channel islands and nearby French ports. Jersey also has the fifth busiest airport in the British Isles, frequent daily services being maintained with the principal airports in the United Kingdom and Eire. Regular air services are also operated between Jersey and the other islands, Paris and other nearby French airports. The airport has fine modern facilities for passengers and freight, and charter services are also available. Flying time to London is less than one hour.

Internally the island has an extensive road system, and a hotel complex commensurate with its status as a leading tourist resort: some measure of its wealth and stability can be gauged from the fact that Jersey has one of the highest population : motor vehicle ratios in the world.

GOVERNMENT

Jersey's Governmental connection with the United Kingdom devolves primarily from the Crown and not from the United Kingdom Government. While in strict law the United Kingdom Parliament can legislate for Jersey in all matters, this has now been limited by usage in respect of taxation and matters of domestic concern to the Island, for which the Island is considered responsible. The United Kingdom Government is however responsible for Jersey's external relations, and has recently completed negotiations with the E.E.C. countries on Jersey's behalf.

The governing body is called the States of Jersey. The States consists of 52 elected members each of whom has voting power, together with the Dean of Jersey, the Attorney General and the Solicitor General. It is presided over by the Bailiff, appointed by the Crown, and this position is in some respects equivalent to that of the Speaker in commonwealth legislation assemblies. Laws passed by the States do not come into effect, except for triennial regulations, until they have been sanctioned by the United Kingdom Monarch in Privy Council. The Queen's representative in the Island, the Lieutenant-Governor, has power of veto over any resolution in the States, but only in respect of such matters as may concern the special interest of the Monarch.

There are no political parties in the accepted sense of the term, and elections are conducted by residents standing on an individual basis.

It can be seen therefore that the Island is in practical terms internally self governing. This state has existed to a greater or lesser extent for a period of over 700 years during which time the present democratic system involving elected members and a universal franchise has evolved.

Law

The laws of the Island of Jersey are based on the ancient customary law of Normandy. This remains the basis of the law today, and in many respects differs substantially from English law. Where needed the laws have been modernized, and although in some respects English procedure is copied and English precedents quoted in the Courts of the Island, nevertheless an independent system of law has been maintained.

Language

English is the primary language used throughout Jersey. In the country districts particularly the old Norman-French language is maintained but today those who learned Norman-French as a first language now also speak English. Legal contracts are, however, written in French, but all legal firms maintain or have access to bilingual staff and translations are readily available.

Currency and Exchange Control

Jersey is part of the sterling area and accordingly this is the currency issued. Jersey currency notes to a value of about £1,500,000 net were in circulation at 31st December, 1967. These are backed by investments in United Kingdom Government Stocks, and deposits at local joint stock and merchant banks.

The United Kingdom Exchange Control Act 1947 was specially extended to include the Channel Islands and the provisions of that Act may be taken as applying also to Jersey. Therefore, exchange control consent whether from an authorized dealer or from the Bank of England, as appropriate, is required in respect of dealings in foreign currency, and in stocks with persons resident outside the Island. The Insular Authorities have agreed that the United Kingdom programme of voluntary restraint with regard to investments in various overseas countries be extended to Jersey. The investment dollar premium surrender requirements are applicable to Jersey based entities and individuals.

Financial and Professional Services

No one should have difficulty in obtaining satisfactory legal advice in Jersey as there are presently in practice over thirty advocates of the Royal Court, and a rather smaller number of qualified solicitors. The leading legal firms in the Island are well acquainted with the problems of new residents and those who wish to set up entities in Jersey and remain domiciled and/or resident elsewhere. There are also currently more than a dozen accounting firms, several of whom have international connections and are accordingly readily able to advise on questions of foreign as well as local taxation. Jersey also has several stockbroking firms who maintain close contacts with other markets in addition to that in London, through which most transactions ultimately pass. A market in various local securities is also maintained by these firms. Various unit trust funds based in the Island are operated on behalf of several of the largest United Kingdom based firms in this field. The major United Kingdom joint stock banks are well represented in Jersey, both in the capital, St. Helier, and in other parts of the Island. The joint stock banks have also formed local subsidiaries to perform executor and trustee services and comparatively recently three such banks have formed merchant banking subsidiaries. Various key United Kingdom and foreign merchant and joint stock banks have either formed local subsidiaries or have taken substantial investment interest in such Jersey based merchant banks. There are also a number of banks and finance houses under locally based ownership.

Banks and financial institutions in Jersey are controlled by a law similar to the United Kingdom Prevention of Fraud (Investment) Act 1958, called the Depositors and Investors (Prevention of Fraud) (General Provisions) (Jersey) Order 1968.

It is apparent, therefore, that Jersey professional firms and other entities are well able to provide advice and information on an extensive basis. The facilities available are constantly being expanded in response to an ever growing demand for the services offered and some indication of the extent to which lawyers, accountants, banks and merchant banks are utilized by non-residents can be determined by considering the number of such bodies, and the wide range of services offered successfully, in an Island where resident population is in the region of 65,000 only.

INTERNAL TAX STRUCTURE

Import duties are levied at comparatively low levels but there are no taxes levied on capital, capital gains or wealth. Neither are any death duties in existence, although assets held abroad by Jersey residents may be liable to duty subject to the laws of the country in which the assets are situated. Taxes on income however do exist and persons resident or ordinarily resident in the Island are liable in respect of all income arising whether in the Island or elsewhere. Non-residents fall liable in respect of all income derived from property and sources in Jersey, on trades, professions and employments exercised in the Island, and on pensions arising in Jersey.

The standard rate of Jersey tax is 0·20p. in the £ (20 per cent), and this has remained constant since 1940. Various personal allowances and reliefs are available to individuals; companies and trusts are chargeable at the standard rate.

Corporation Tax (Duty)

A company registered in Jersey, but not controlled from Jersey (all directors' meetings and all trading of such a company must take place outside the Island, beneficial ownership must be outside Jersey and the United Kingdom) is only liable to Jersey corporation duty of £200 per annum. The Jersey registered external company may gain relief from this corporation tax in any year if (*a*) it opts to pay income tax on all profits whether remitted or not, (*b*) it satisfies the Comptroller of Income Tax that no income tax would be payable were the company resident. Note, however, that a Jersey registered company controlled outside Jersey may also be liable to income tax in the country from which it is controlled. This will, of course, depend on the particular country's income tax legislation.

It is now agreed that if external companies carry on all business and transactions outside Jersey, there is no need to prove that management is outside the Island, but all board meetings must be held outside Jersey.

Jersey income tax law now contains provision against legal avoidance of local income tax, whereby if the Comptroller is of the opinion that the main purpose or one of the main purposes of a transaction is the avoidance or lawful reduction of the liability of any person to income tax, the Comptroller may make such assessment or additional assessment as he considers appropriate to counteract such avoidance.

Stamp Duties

It should be noted that no stamp duty is levied in Jersey in respect of the transfer of movable property within the Island: movable property is deemed to include the transfer of stocks and shares. Duty is payable on the formation of a company calculated on the total authorized capital, or increase therein, at a rate of £10 for the first £8,000 authorized capital, or part thereof and 0·12½p. per £100 thereafter. Fees are also payable on the sale or transfer of immovable *i.e.* heritable property, and *inter alia*, on contracts.

Withholding Tax

While Jersey has no separate withholding tax, tax at the standard rate of 0·20p. in the pound is deductible from all dividends payable by Jersey corporate bodies. (By concession, this withholding tax need not be paid by external companies.) This is recoverable, or partially recoverable by a British subject wherever he may reside, on the basis of a proportional allowances claim in the proportion that his Jersey income bears to his world income. In strict law, Jersey non-residents are liable to Jersey income tax on bank interest arising in the Island but, by concession, this bank interest is payable gross to a non-resident, and is not generally assessed to Jersey tax where it is the only income arising to him in the Island. (This concession is not extended to corporate bodies registered in Jersey, or the estates of deceased persons in respect of income arising after death.)

Tax Treaties

Jersey has reciprocal double taxation relief agreements with Guernsey (including Alderney and Herm) and with the United Kingdom. There is also a restricted agreement with France, concerning solely the exemption of profits from the operating of ships and aircraft of their respective undertakings.

The agreements between Jersey and the United Kingdom and Jersey/Guernsey provide that the respective taxation authorities shall exchange such information as is necessary for the carrying out of the provisions of the respective arrangements or for the prevention of fraud or the administration of statutory provisions against legal avoidance in relation to the taxes which are the subject of the arrangements. The arrangements tend to follow the general pattern of double taxation agreements made by the United Kingdom and the present agreement with Jersey states *inter alia* that the profits of a Jersey enterprise shall not be subject to a United Kingdom Tax, unless that enterprise is engaged in business in the United Kingdom through a permanent establishment therein. A permanent establishment is defined as a branch management or other fixed place of business, but does not include an agency unless the agent habitually exercises a general authority to negotiate and conclude contracts on behalf of such enterprise or has a stock of merchandise from which he regularly fills orders on its behalf.

The agreement does not provide for any credit relief for United Kingdom/Guernsey residents in respect of dividends and debenture interest from Jersey resident companies, or vice versa; but the parties may nevertheless avail themselves of unilateral relief under the domestic laws concerned.

Available Entities

It is possible that more than one of the basic Jersey entities be used in any one operation. The commonly operated legal structures include:

(*a*) Jersey registered companies comprising trading companies, and investment holding or dealing companies;
(*b*) Jersey registered companies controlled outside Jersey;
(*c*) discretionary trusts;
(*d*) partnerships.

The Company

Companies registered in Jersey may only be formed with limited liability and there is no distinction between public and private companies. However it is possible for a Jersey registered company to obtain a quotation on a recognized stock exchange.

(i) *Trading Companies*

Apart from the obvious usefulness of this type of entity to a resident, these may be formed for and on behalf of a non-resident either for the purpose of trading within the Island or for handling trading transactions to and from external sources.

(ii) *Investment Holding Companies*

These companies, as the name implies, hold investments for the purpose of earning income and if profits on the occasional realization of investments are incidental to the main purpose, those profits will not be assessed to Jersey income tax. A person resident and domiciled in Jersey is generally permitted to form such a company to hold investments anywhere in the world, providing that he has been so resident for a period of two to three years, and the formation of the company will not enable existing liabilities to taxation in the United Kingdom to be avoided. A resident for less than this period may usually only form an investment company without power in the memorandum to invest in the United Kingdom. It should be noted here that under the provisions of Jersey company law the memorandum of association may only be altered as to the name of the company, or to increase the authorized share capital.

(iii) *Investment Dealing Companies*

The business of these companies is primarily dealing in investments and both the dealing profits, less losses, as well as investment income are subject to income tax.

Companies Controlled Within Jersey

A Jersey resident company is liable to income tax on its assessed profits at the standard rate of 0·20p. in the £1. There is no profits tax, corporation tax or capital gains tax. Dividends are paid under deduction of standard rate tax.

Jersey limited liability companies must be registered in the Royal Court of Jersey. Provided the memorandum and articles of association do not limit trading, and neither the States Treasury nor the Bank of England have placed restriction on the activities of the company, it is free to trade as it wishes, subject to its obtaining exchange control permission to involve itself in activities outside the sterling area. There is no general bar covering nationality of directors, although as far as a Jersey registered company is concerned control and administration must be exercised in Jersey. The company must initially have three founder members each subscribing for a minimum of three shares of £1 each, and must hold its directors' and general meetings in the Island. The company must hold an annual general meeting of shareholders each year. The holding of such meetings is governed by the articles of association as are voting rights, but the statutory provisions operate where these are silent.

The company must also maintain a registered office in the Island and complete an annual return of shareholders made up to 1st January each year to be delivered to the Judicial Greffier of the Island by 31st January. This annual return of shareholders is available for public inspection. A register of members must be maintained at the registered office and must be available for public inspection during certain hours of each business day. Each company is required to have its full name inscribed on its public office and on its stationery. A company must also have a company seal inscribed with its full name. There is no provision in law for a Jersey registered company to make its minutes available for public inspection, nor is it obliged to list the names of directors on notepaper or stationery. But the directors or managers of the company are required to keep records of the company's transactions and also of its correspondence.

The annual maintenance cost of a Jersey registered company varies in accordance with the required services. Where only a registered office is kept in the Island and minimum services in accordance with statute are required a nominal annual fee in the region of £250 might be negotiated. However there is no standard and such fees, together with remuneration of local directors, are a matter of negotiation in each case.

Where an individual or an entity outside the sterling area wishes to participate in a company, Bank of England permission is required for the external source to take up its interest in the Jersey entity. In that case some restriction may be placed on the repatriation of capital and the future activities and capitalization of the Jersey entity. It is of course possible, if all beneficial owners are sterling area non-residents, for the company to maintain an external account. It is also possible for an externally owned company to have a share capital in a currency other than sterling. In establishing such a company, care should of course be exercised at the outset to ensure that the non-Jersey participants do not infringe the regulations existing in their countries of residence with regard to the transfer of assets and dealings abroad.

Formation of an orthodox Jersey company should take a period of about three weeks to one month. Where the provisions of memorandum and articles of association are unusual a longer period would be required depending upon the extent of the variation from normal. When exchange control permission is required, formation is liable to take a period of months, although once permission had been obtained the time element would be no greater than that aforementioned. Costs are partially dependent upon scale fees payable according to the amount of authorized capital, but a minimum size company with a capital of say £100 with a standard memorandum and articles of association would cost approximately £120 to £150 to form.

Companies Controlled Outside Jersey

Companies may be registered in Jersey with the place of control situate outside Jersey. The advantage of such a company is that, from the Jersey income tax point of view, the only tax payable in Jersey would be a corporation tax of £200 per annum. It is necessary to establish to the satisfaction of the Comptroller of Income Tax in Jersey, that the control and central management of the company is, in fact, outside Jersey, and all directors' meetings must be held in the country of control. The Comptroller of Income Tax will generally accept that the control of the company is outside Jersey in the case of an investment holding company, or an investment dealing company, if the beneficial owner of such a company is resident outside Jersey and outside the United Kingdom.

In the case of a trading company he will not accept that the company is controlled from outside Jersey if the beneficial owners of the company are resident either in Jersey or the United Kingdom, and he will require full details of the company's activities to ensure that the company is, in fact, trading from outside Jersey. The company must maintain a registered office of the company in Jersey but only secretarial matters may be dealt with from that office. If it is possible to establish the seat of control of a company which fulfils the requirements stated above in a place which has no income tax, the corporation tax paid would be the only tax suffered by the company—apart, of course, from any withholding tax deducted from the company's dividend income.

The formation of a company described above will follow the same procedure as that outlined in the case of a normal Jersey company and application will be made to the Comptroller of Income Tax to have the company accepted as a "corporation tax" company. The residence of the individual directors of such a company does not determine the place of control, but it is not unusual to find one or more of the directors resident in the country of control.

The Trust

Jersey is an extremely popular place for the setting up of trusts.

Non-Jersey trust income is not subject to Jersey tax provided that (*a*) the beneficiaries are not residents of Jersey, and (*b*) the controller of taxes gives his approval at the time the trust is formed.

Considerable care must be exercised in the setting up of any trust in Jersey as the law of trusts has not developed in the Island to the extent it has in other jurisdictions and in particular no statute law on trusts exists.

The settlor need not be a Jersey resident; however it is necessary that the trustees appointed be resident in the Island. As Jersey has no statute law on trusts it is imperative that the trust deed be sufficiently comprehensive to provide for all foreseeable contingencies. The trust may be set up either to hold the settled assets direct, or indirectly, for example through a Jersey registered company, controlled outside Jersey, which would hold the relevant assets. Income may be accumulated during the whole of the period of the trust; that and the payment of income and capital is generally left at the absolute discretion of the trustees. The settlor may furnish the trustees with a letter of intent to which the trustees may, but are not bound to, have regard.

It is also normal for a protector to be appointed who can be a friend of the settlor or beneficiaries and who can have power to approve or veto any action of the trustees.

Formation costs of such a trust should, if it was designed in simple form, not necessarily exceed £150, this being additional to the cost of any related legal entity, and assuming that principles have previously been agreed would take a minimum of two to three weeks to set up. It must be noted however that a very wide variation in detailed purposes and requirements is encountered in practice and accordingly it follows that a consequent wide variation in costs occurs. Regard must also be had to the exchange control regulations relevant to the Island as previously stated in this chapter.

The Partnership

Non-residents, either individuals or corporate bodies, may enter into partnership with Jersey residents or Jersey registered companies for the purpose of either trading within the Island or throughout the world. Such partnerships must be of a commercial nature and the partnership must be proven to be based in Jersey. The business must be carried on from Jersey and the profits of the partnership will be subject to Jersey income tax at 0·20p. in the £1.

Although it is not necessary in strict law, the partners would probably require a partnership deed to be made to regulate the workings of the partnership. Costs and time required to formulate such a deed are obviously dependent upon the degree of complexity of the requirements of the various partners; however in a comparatively simple case, legal fees and attendances could account for approximately £100 in addition to the cost of obtaining professional advice as to the best method of meeting the said requirements.

There is no broad restriction as to the nationality of partners, although exchange control permission would be required for the participation of non-sterling area partners and this control would also be required in regard to certain trading outside the sterling area. The annual maintenance cost of such an entity would be utterly dependent upon the nature and extent of the trading of the partnership.

Should the business name of the partnership not consist of the surnames of all partners who are individuals and the corporate names of all partners who are bodies corporate without any addition, other than christian names or initials of individual partners, registration will be required in accordance with the Registration of Business Names (Jersey) Law. Registration fees are however minimal.

LIBERIA

THE INTERNATIONAL TRUST COMPANY OF LIBERIA

The Republic of Liberia, located on the West Coast of Africa, was proclaimed in 1847 and has had a stable government since its formation.

The country has a land area of over 43,000 square miles and a population of over 1,000,000.

The principal exports of the country are rubber, high quality iron ore, diamonds, palm kernels, and coffee. The large-scale, long-term developments in rubber and iron ore by foreign interests assist in providing a highly favourable balance of trade to Liberia.

In recent years Liberian trade has dramatically expanded due to a healthy government attitude towards private investment. Though jealously guarding her sovereignty, Liberia has welcomed foreign interests and realizes that by offering and rigidly guaranteeing equitable rights to overseas investors, she can develop her resources to the full.

Liberia maintains its own diplomatic and consular representation in most of the important nations of the world and at the United Nations.

COMMUNICATIONS

Liberia enjoys ready accessibility to centres of world commerce. The free port of Monrovia is one of the most modern ports on the West Coast of Africa. This port is served by major steamship lines operating from Europe, the United States and the Far East. Secondary ports at Buchanan, Cape Palmas and Sinoe serve Liberia's growing coastal and internal trade.

Liberia's principal international airport at Robertsfield, outside Monrovia, is served on regular direct air schedules from the United States and Europe.

Air mail service between Liberia and major world cities is generally good.

Government

The government is patterned after the government of the United States, with a bicameral legislature consisting of a Senate and House of Representatives.

Language

The official language of commerce and government is English.

Currency and Exchange Control

The U.S. dollar is legal tender in Liberia. Liberian coins circulate interchangeably with U.S. coins in units up to $1·00.

There is no exchange control whatsoever.

Financial and Professional Services

Competent corporation and admiralty attorneys are available. Several European and American accounting firms maintain branches in Liberia. The banks, usually branches or affiliates of American, European and Lebanese banks, provide a full range of banking facilities and investment advice.

Internal Tax Structure

Liberia has a modern tax law designed to attract foreign incorporations. Under this law Liberian corporations do not incur income tax liabilities in Liberia:

(*a*) if more than 50 per cent of the corporate stock is held by non-Liberians, and
(*b*) if corporate income is derived from sources outside Liberia.

Tax Treaties

The Republic of Liberia is in the process of studying the negotiation of tax treaties with several countries.

The Corporation

Advantages

The principal advantages which attorneys and management recognize when selecting Liberia as a corporate domicile are:

1. *Convenient domicile requirements*
   (*a*) Directors, officers, stockbrokers and incorporators may be of any nationality and may reside anywhere.
   (*b*) Meetings of stockholders, directors, or incorporators may be held anywhere in the world—by proxy if desired.
   (*c*) The corporation's executive office, where its records are kept, may be located in any country.
   (*d*) The connection the corporation need have with Liberia is simplified by the use of a trust company in Liberia as statutory resident business agent in Liberia.

2. *Anonymity*
   (*a*) All or part of the stock issue may be in the form of registered or bearer shares.
   (*b*) After incorporation, any change of officers and directors need not be recorded in a public register.
   (*c*) The resident business agent is not required to file any reports with the Government regarding corporate activities.

3. *Income tax*
   There is no income tax.

4. *Rapid formation*
   (*a*) Using one of the model charter forms, corporate existence is usually obtained within 48 hours.

(b) If an attorney drafts his own charter, corporate existence can normally be obtained within two business days after arrival of papers in Liberia.

(c) In any case, a cable from Liberia will advise the date of corporate existence of the new corporation which can then be organized and transact business.

5. *No translations*

The cost and delay for translations of corporate documents is eliminated.

6. *Reasonable costs*

(a) Upon incorporation—

Payable to the Liberian Government:

capitalization tax	minimum	$100
stamp and miscellaneous fees	approximately	15
Formation costs; includes $150 for first year as resident business agent		500
	Total	$615

(b) After incorporation, annually on the corporation's anniversary date—

Corporation registration fee (payable to the Liberian Government)		$100
Statutory resident business agent's fee		150
	Total	$250

There are no other mandatory fees or charges either upon incorporation or later.

7. *Minimum capital requirements*

The minimum capital required is $500, or its equivalent in foreign currency at the legal rate of exchange.

8. *Absence of currency restrictions*

9. *Good communications*

10. *Stability of government*

Formation

Three or more persons, the incorporators, may organize a Liberian corporation by signing a certificate of incorporation which is filed with the Secretary of State. Incorporators may be of any nationality and may reside anywhere.

Contents of the certificate of incorporation

Liberian corporation law specifies certain provisions which the certificate of incorporation must include:

(*a*) *Name.* The name of the corporation and the nature of business to be transacted; the words or abbreviation to indicate that it is a corporation, for example:

Corporation	Company
Limited	Limitada
Societe Anonyme	Societe par actions
Sociedad Anonima	Aktiengesellschaft
Corp.	Inc.
Ltd.	Ltda.
S.A.	A.G.

The name of the corporation may be written in any language.

(*b*) *Capitalization.* A statement of the maximum number of shares of capital stock which the corporation is authorized to issue. This number may be changed by amendment to the certificate of incorporation. The board of directors may issue any amount up to the maximum authorized. Capital of Liberian corporations may be expressed in any currency. Shares may have par value or may be nominal and without par value. Par value shares may be authorized for issue by the board of directors at par or any value above par, for instance, at the market price. The board of directors may not issue par value shares for less than par value. Shares without par value may be issued at any value set by the board of directors at the time of issuance, and no value is stated for them either in the certificate of incorporation or on the face of the share certificates.

Bearer shares may be authorized and issued, provided they are fully paid.

Provision may be made for stock of different classes, with different preference rights as to dividends, voting, *etc.*

(*c*) *Initial capital.* A statement of the amount of capital with which the corporation will begin business which must be at least $500 or its equivalent in any foreign currency paid in before commencing business (calculated at the official rate of exchange with U.S. dollars).

(*d*) *Existence.* A statement whether the corporation is to have perpetual existence or whether its existence is to expire at a definite date.

(*e*) *Domicile.* The domicile of the corporation is Monrovia, Liberia. The certificate of incorporation should also specify the name and domicile of the corporation's resident business agent. The corporation need not be present in Liberia in any other way than through the presence of its statutory resident business agent. The company does not need to carry on operations in Liberia.

(*f*) *Directors.* The names and addresses of the original directors. The corporation must begin existence with at least three directors. There is no nationality requirement for directors of Liberian corporations. Original directors can be provided by the trust company undertaking the incorporation. It is the practice to make no additional charge for this service, and to cause the directors to return their resignations with the certificate of incorporation.

A maximum and minimum number of directors is usually stated in the charter thus allowing the board of directors to expand and contract as business requires without amending the certificate of incorporation.

(*g*) *Incorporators.* The names and addresses of the incorporators who subscribe the certificate of incorporation, and the number of shares each agrees to take. Incorporators are provided at no additional cost by the trust company which undertakes the incorporation, and their transfers of subscription will be returned with the certificate of incorporation.

(*h*) *Special provisions.* A provision stating whether or not the officers and directors of the company, its subsidiaries, and other persons who have served at the request of the corporation, shall be indemnified for expenses incurred in connection with the defence of any action brought against them for having acted on behalf of the corporation (see exact terms in section 2(j) of the Liberian Corporation Law).

The certificate of incorporation may include any special provisions which are desired regarding the scope of activities or conduct of the affairs of the corporation which are not contrary to the Liberian Corporation Law.

Standard incorporation procedure

Attorneys may form Liberian corporations directly with a trust company or through its correspondents.

(*a*) The original of the certificate of incorporation, submitted by an attorney, must be signed by the incorporators. Their signatures must be acknowledged before an authorized official or notary public located in the country where the certificate is signed. If the certificate is executed outside Liberia, the signature of the public official or notary public should be authenticated by a Liberian consul. In practice it is much more convenient to have the trust company provide incorporators as mentioned above. This eliminates the requirement for authentication by a local notary and Liberian consul.

(*b*) The signed and acknowledged original and four signed copies should be airmailed to the trust company concerned. If certified copies are desired, additional copies should be furnished.

(*c*) Corporate existence is usually obtained within two business days after arrival of papers in Liberia. Cable advice of existence is sent by the trust company.

(*d*) When processing has been completed, the trust company will return the approved original of the certificate of incorporation and related papers.

Accelerated incorporation procedure

Liberian corporations may be formed within 48 hours using authorized model certificates of incorporation. Using these models (minor changes may be made), incorporation procedures can be completed by the trust company undertaking the incorporation upon receipt of cabled instructions from one of its correspondents outside of Liberia.

Ship Registration

In December 1948, Liberia adopted a modern Maritime Code, and Liberia now has the largest merchant fleet in the world. Most of this tonnage represents major-sized new construction. The Maritime Code permits both expeditous registration of a vessel and its efficient operation thereafter. Certificates of registration are issued by the Commissioner or a Deputy Commissioner of Maritime Affairs of the Republic of Liberia after approval by the Maritime Administrator.

A member of the Inter-Governmental Maritime Consultative Organization, Liberia is also a signatory of major maritime conventions (including Safety of Life at Sea 1960) which require ship operators to maintain high standards of seamanship.

LIECHTENSTEIN

ALLGEMEINES TREUUNTERNEHMEN

Liechtenstein is a mountainous country, lying on the right bank of the Rhine between Switzerland and Austria. It is some 16 miles long and averages about 3·7 miles wide.

Communications

Communication by air is via Zurich, Switzerland. Main line trains to Vienna stop at Buchs, from which it is a short journey by road to Vaduz, the capital city. Post and cable communication is excellent: Liechtenstein is linked to the European "Direct Dial" telephone system.

Government

The principality of Liechtenstein is a constitutional, hereditary monarchy on democratic and parliamentary bases: the power of the state is inherent in and issues from the Prince and the people and is exercised by both of them pursuant to the provisions of the Constitution. This is laid down in section 2 of the Constitution of 1921 at present in force. This constitutional article defines the political character of the Principality. Accordingly, Liechtenstein is fundamentally a combination of a monarchy and a democracy. In exercising their rights, both parties, the Prince and the people, must co-operate pursuant to the Constitution, which provides for a division of powers or for joint action.

Liechtenstein, impoverished after World War I as a customs partner of Austria, has since the 1920s done its utmost to promote public welfare. Originally a poor agricultural state, it has developed into one of the most highly industrialized states, which owes its present prosperity and wealth to the determination and the working ardour of the people, the intelligent state government and planning, the customs union with

Switzerland, the stable economic association with Switzerland, and not least, to the open-minded legislation and the modern and differentiated codification of its own individual and corporate law, which not only provides for its own forms of association, but also recognizes the forms known to the legal system of other states.

The reasons which lead to the formation of holding and domiciliary companies in Liechtenstein are manifold and by no means always entirely taxational. For one thing, Liechtenstein benefits by its central situation in Europe, its sound economic position, the hard Swiss currency and the stable political situation. For another, many businessmen and business organizations, seeing the European economic area divided between Common Market and E.F.T.A., have decided to consolidate their plants in those two areas in organizational respects, and then, for reasons of financial policy, to direct or supervise them through a Liechtenstein holding or domiciliary company, or to appoint the Liechtenstein holding or domiciliary company as an intermediary or an adjusting buffer.

LAW

Until the end of the 1914–1918 World War, Liechtenstein was closely associated with Austria-Hungary. It applied the Austrian Civil Law. After the First World War, however, a customs' agreement was concluded with Switzerland—a country which stands much closer to Liechtenstein both from the territorial and from the economic point of view.

Nevertheless, Liechtenstein did not adopt the Swiss Civil Code but has rather tended to complement the Austrian laws by legislation of its own. In view of the restricted size of the country, which does not admit of the development of original legal thinking, the whole of Liechtenstein's legislation is influenced by German jurisprudence. The legislature did not however hesitate to go its own way. A code of property law, which is a replica of the Swiss, has been in force since 1923 and in 1926 Liechtenstein adopted new legislation of its own, the so-called P.G.R. code (*Personen- und Gesellschaftsrecht*) *i.e.* the law concerning physical and juridical persons.

The P.G.R. is the third part of the Code of Civil Law. It comprises an introduction, Parts 1 to 5 and the Final Part. The parts are divided into Titles, Sections and Articles, while the Final Part is divided into

Paragraphs. Part 1 deals with individuals (physical persons); Part 2 with associations of persons (juridical persons) *e.g.* the establishment, the company limited by shares, the foundation, the trust; Part 3 with the association without juridical personality (communities governed by the law concerning physical persons); Part 4 deals with particular forms of endowment and with the ordinary partnership; finally Part 5 deals with the Official Register, the names of firms and business book-keeping. The fiduciary enterprise (the commercial trust) is dealt with in Article 932a added in 1928, comprising 170 paragraphs and forming Section 2 under Title 16 of Part 4. Part 2, Title 5 deals with establishments and foundations. The provisions concerning establishments are to be found in paragraphs 534 to 551.

The definition of the holding company and the domiciliary company is a definition of the Tax Statute. This (in the version of 4th June, 1963) provides in s. 83, para. 1 that a holding company is any registered corporation whose objects consist entirely or mainly in property management, participation in other business organizations or permanent management of holdings in such. A company coming under this definition is exempt from property tax and earnings tax or profit tax, and is merely liable to capital tax at the rate of one per thousand of the paid-up capital and reserves (total capital invested); the minimum capital tax payable, however, is 600 francs per annum.

The law defines the domiciliary company in section 84 (version of 4th June, 1963) as any registered corporation which merely has its domicile in Liechtenstein, but is not economically active in the country; however, it may keep an office of its own in Liechtenstein and direct its business from Liechtenstein. Domiciliary companies are exempt from property tax and earnings tax or profit tax and are merely liable to capital taxation at the rate of one per thousand of the paid-up capital and reserves (total capital invested); the minimum capital tax payable, however, is 600 francs per annum.

Whilst registration in the Commercial Register is compulsory for holding and domiciliary companies (besides the legal qualification as a corporate body) the so-called foundations need not be registered in order to obtain tax privileges similar to those granted to holding and domiciliary companies. Foundations, including family foundations, pay capital tax at the same rate as do holding and domiciliary companies, save however that the rate is reduced if the foundation capital exceeds 2 million francs or 10 million francs respectively. Thus, the foundation pays an annual tax at the rate of one per thousand on a capital up to

2 million, 0·75 per thousand on a capital ranging from 2 million to 10 million and 0·50 per thousand on a capital over 10 million.

Another point worth mentioning here is that Liechtenstein, like Switzerland, enforces bank secrecy. The Liechtenstein Bank Law provides heavy sanctions for any breach of professional secrecy.

Language

The language of the country is German, but English is commonly used in commercial transactions and widely spoken and understood in the business and professional community.

Currency and Exchange Control

The currency is the Swiss franc. There is no exchange control.

Financial and Professional Services

Lawyers, accountants, banks and trust companies are available with experience in dealing with the affairs of clients from other countries.

Internal Tax Structure

Liechtenstein has taxes on capital and on income which affect persons resident or doing business in the country. However, companies and other entities (as indicated below) enjoy substantial tax privileges so long as they are not doing active business in the Principality.

Tax Treaties

Liechtenstein has not concluded double taxation agreements with any country except Austria.

Available Entities

The Establishment

The establishment is a new type of juridical person in Liechtenstein law (P.G.R.). It has evolved from the institutions of administrative law and more particularly from institutions found in actual practice. The establishment is half-way between the corporation and the foundation and, consequently, it may be formed either with or without associates. The additional regulations enacted on this subject are inspired by the provisions concerning co-operative societies and the principles governing foundations.

The establishment is an enterprise, legally independent and lawfully organized, devoted to the pursuit of lasting economic or other aims, entered in the register of establishments of the Official Register, which has its own assets and which is neither an institution of public law nor a juridical person of any other kind.

According to the legal definition, an establishment is a legally independent enterprise. Consequently it should have a juridical personality of its own just as a company limited by shares or other form of juridical person. Moreover it must be provided with an organization of its own, enabling it to act as an independent juridical person and conveying to it rights both active and passive. An establishment may not be set up to serve some temporary economic purpose rapidly attained; the law does not set any limit as to the period of time required for the achievement of the lasting economic purposes pursued. On the contrary, there is no doubt that as a form of enterprise provided with an organization of its own, an establishment should seek to attain objectives of a lasting nature and not merely temporary ones. As an economic form of enterprise, the establishment requires material (and generally also human) resources: it is normally endowed by its founder with a capital designed to secure the attainment of its economic purpose.

The law provides that individuals, firms, groups or juridical persons whether otherwise entered in the Official Register or not, may found an establishment and may also act as directors of the establishment. Only one founder is required. The law does not set any requirements as to the founder's nationality or domicile. This means that anybody who fulfils the legal requirements and complies with the provisions of the law may found an establishment in Liechtenstein. The establishment may also be set up through power of attorney and, of course, by a fiduciary on behalf of third persons.

To found an establishment it is necessary to draw up articles of incorporation signed by the founder. His signature must be officially authenticated or legalized by a notary.

The articles of incorporation must contain the following information:

(1) name of the establishment;
(2) purpose of the establishment and the particular objects of its proposed activity;
(3) capital of the establishment;
(4) organization and organs;
(5) principles governing the accounts and balance sheet and method of publication of notices;
(6) provisions concerning the liquidation and dissolution of the establishment.

As for the name of the establishment, the wording in the different languages must tally as to substance. According to general practice, the term "*Anstalt*" is translated as "*Etablissement*" in French "Establishment" in English and "*Stabilimento*" in Italian—a translation faithful in the literal sense but not to the concept. The law however requires a truthful name and any fancy designations used may not be untrue, immoral or illegal or contribute to unfair competition in any way. Statements for mere publicity purposes may not be included in the name of an establishment, nor may sub-titles.

An establishment need not be profit-making. It may also serve to achieve purposes of public usefulness. (The pursuit of public usefulness aims is, of course, the particular concern of establishments governed by public law.) The objects need not in any way be of an economic nature, nor is it necessary for the establishment to run commercial or industrial undertakings in the country. For instance, it may hold financial interests exclusively in foreign firms or exercise certain controlling rights over them.

The objects of the undertaking may be drafted freely. The wording may be in either broad or precise terms and their description is left to the founder, but the articles must be amended should the objects be changed or amplified. Too broad a formulation often conceals the actual object of the enterprise.

The law does not prescribe any fixed currency for the capital an establishment should have, but only minimum requirements. The minimum capital and, accordingly, the minimum assets, must represent 20,000 francs for establishments without participation shares or associates' rights and 50,000 francs for establishments with participation shares. The minimum capital and the corresponding minimum assets must be fully paid in or contributed.

Participation shares are permitted but in the overwhelming majority of cases the capital of the establishment is neither divided nor divisible. In such cases, the capital as a whole carries all the benefit to be derived of the establishment. The investor or the beneficiary, *i.e.* the founder of the establishment or his legal successor may obviously include in the articles special or general provisions with regard to the allotment of net profits. As the supreme authority of the establishment, the founder or the beneficiary entitled to act in his place has at all times the power to alter the articles in this or any other respect, to complement them, to amplify or to restrict them.

The question of the division of capital into participation shares is above all a fiscal one, due to the coupon tax of 3 per cent on distributed profits.

The liabilities of an establishment are guaranteed solely by its assets.

The organs of the establishment are as follows:

The founder or his legal successor. The founder or his legal successor, (or the founders or their legal successors) are the supreme authority of an establishment.

Board of directors. The Board of directors may consist of one or several members. One member has to be domiciled in Liechtenstein.

Auditors. The founder may make provision for the auditing of the accounts in the articles of incorporation or at any time later and define the scope of the auditing, either in general terms or with reference to special cases.

Legal representation. For companies which do not carry on any activities in Liechtenstein (*Sitzgesellschaften*) and for holding companies, the legal representatives constitute a further organ of the company which is empowered to represent the company, not to third parties, but to the authorities of the country in so far as it may receive from them communications, instructions and orders destined to the company and may safeguard the interests of the company represented in relation to the authorities. Apart from this, the legal representatives may only bind the company, if specifically empowered to that effect.

Duty and tax

An establishment is liable to pay a formation duty amounting to 2 per cent of the establishment's capital.

The registration fees in the Commercial Register amount to 200 francs for a capital of 100,000 francs and 50 francs for each additional 100,000 francs plus stamp duties.

Establishments which carry on activities within the country are liable to pay taxes on their capital and on their profits. The tax on capital amounts to 0·2 per cent of the capital and reserves. The taxes on profits vary between 7·5 per cent and 15 per cent, that is half the percentage of the net profit in relation to the assessable taxable capital, 7·5 per cent being the minimum and 15 per cent the maximum taxation rate. If the establishment does not engage in any economic activities within the country (*Sitzgesellschaft*), it is not liable to pay tax on the profits. Such an establishment is only liable to pay 0·1 per cent on capital and reserves with a minimum of 600 francs per annum. This tax is payable each year in advance. If the establishment has a divided-up capital, it has to pay the 3 per cent coupon tax on the earnings distributed, in addition to the other taxes. The tax authorities are entitled to inspect the book-keeping of all corporate bodies; the establishment and all other companies with divided-up capital are liable, however, to submit their balance sheet and profit and loss account every year to the tax authorities.

The Company Limited by Shares

The company limited by shares (hereinafter called simply "corporation") is defined as an association which has a name of its own and whose pre-determined capital is divided into shares and for whose commitments only the association's assets are liable.

The capital may also be divided into fractions or quotas (instead of shares), in which case it is by law necessary to specify, besides the quotas, the sum of the capital and the reserves in words. Shares with and without par value may be issued concurrently. A special form of the corporation is the corporation with variable capital.

The shares may be of the registered type or of the bearer type, and a corporation may have both types concurrently. As regards the possibility and mode of converting registered shares into bearer shares and vice versa, the articles must contain special provisions. Bearer shares can be issued only against payment of the amount specified in the articles, which must be at least half the face value.

The articles must by law state the following:

(1) name and registered office of the corporation;
(2) objects of the corporation;
(3) amounts of the initial capital and of the individual shares, and whether these are registered shares or bearer shares; nature and amount of the paid-up capital or of the sum paid up on each share;
(4) mode of calling the general meeting, exercising the voting power and passing resolutions;
(5) governing bodies of the corporation and mode of representation;
(6) form of notices to shareholders and outsiders.

Besides these statutory minimum contents, the articles may and should contain further provisions. Such additional particulars are necessary notably in cases of non-cash contributions, special awards to the founders (founders' privileges), as well as in cases where it is decided to depart from the statutory provisions regarding amendment of the articles, enlargement of the scope of business, increase of capital, reduction of capital, and merger. Beyond this, it is convenient to include special provisions which are important to the particular business, such as limitation of the life of the business or prohibition of the transfer of registered shares or restrictions on transfer, voting power, right of representation, etc.

There are two modes of formation, *viz.* the simultaneous procedure and the successive procedure. In the simultaneous procedure, all the founders declare by a memorandum signed by them that they incorporate the corporation, sanction the articles of the corporation, and confirm their acceptance of all the shares by payment. In the successive procedure, the founders do not themselves subscribe for all the shares to be issued under the articles, but instead invite outsiders to participate in the business. The founders lay down and sign the articles, subscribe for some of the shares, and invite the public to subscribe for the rest. Finally, a general meeting of the share subscribers is called to resolve on the acceptance of the subscriptions and the payments made, as well as on the appointment of the officers of the corporation and the ratification of the articles. When, under the successive procedure the public is invited to subscribe for shares, the founders issue a prospectus, which must state the necessary particulars, notably as regards the contents of the articles, the time for subscription and payment, the subscription offices, the issue price of the shares, and the amount payable on the shares by the date of the general meeting.

The minimum payment on the share capital specified is 20 per cent on each share, but the absolute minimum total must be 50,000 francs, which must be fully paid up. If it is decided to accept non-cash contributions or to grant certain shareholders special privileges, the founders must issue a report in writing, setting out the reasons for, and the appropriateness of, the privileges granted to the founders, and the value of the non-cash contributions. The report must be available for inspection at each subscription office at the very beginning of the time given for subscription. Shareholders representing at least one-tenth of the initial capital are entitled to request that the non-cash contributions be valued by experts, and that a neutral report be made on the founders' privileges, in which case such report must be submitted to a second general meeting. If an experts' report has already been submitted to the general meeting, but the subscribers reject it, they are entitled to have their contributions refunded and withdraw, without any claim to indemnify. If the public has been invited to subscribe, the non-cash contributions and the founders' privileges must be sanctioned by a majority of three-quarters of the votes represented in person or by proxy.

When the statutory requirements of the successive procedure or the simultaneous procedure are complete, the corporation must be entered in the Commercial Register.

The capital of the corporation can be in Swiss currency or in any other internationally recognized currency. The statutory minimum capital is 50,000 francs (or its equivalent) and must be fully paid up to that amount. Also in the case of the corporation with variable capital, the capital must never drop below the statutory minimum of 50,000 francs.

The articles may provide for the issue of profit-sharing certificates of a negotiable nature in favour of the founders or even outsiders. Such certificates do not confer upon their holders any membership of the corporation, but simply a conditional creditor's claim to a share of the net profit or of the liquidation proceeds or a right to take up new shares. Such a right to take up new shares must never relate to more than half the shares to be newly issued.

Corporations with variable capital can only issue registered shares, and the corporation's capital can be increased by issuing new shares to established shareholders or to outsiders, or reduced by repayment on shares. The articles of a corporation with variable capital must state the maximum amount to which the capital may be increased, and the minimum amount to which it may be reduced. However, the minimum amount must always be one-tenth of the maximum capital and must never drop below the absolute minimum of 50,000 francs or its equivalent.

Repayment of capital can only be effected on the basis of a liquidation balance sheet showing that, after repayment, the liabilities of the corporation are still covered by the remaining capital, the reserves and the available assets. The mode of repayment must be specified in the articles.

The corporation with variable capital is permitted to keep and also later re-issue the repurchased shares, but while such shares are lying with the corporation, the membership rights attaching thereto must not be asserted. With the corporation with variable capital, at least 10 per cent of the net profit must be allocated to the reserve fund until this reaches the level of the minimum capital specified in the articles.

The corporation may be dissolved by operation of law or in accordance with a provision in the articles or by resolution of a general meeting. Dissolution may also be brought about by judicial order or by bankruptcy. If the objects are unlawful or immoral, the business is deprived of its legal substratum and is therefore by law dissolved.

The corporation must properly keep books, for which the Board is responsible. The balance sheet with the profit and loss account must be submitted for approval to the general meeting within six months of the close of the accounting year. Corporations with a capital exceeding one million francs, and firms issuing unsecured debentures to bearer may be requested by the Government to publish their balance sheets together with the profit and loss accounts. However, this provision does not apply to so-called domiciliary and family-owned corporations.

Duty and tax

At a time not later than the point of registration, the corporation must pay issue duty on the shares. This duty works out at 2 per cent of the paid capital and one per cent of the unpaid capital. The fraction of the total issue duty devolving on each share is rounded up to the next 10 cents, and the minimum duty payable on each share is 10 cents.

The registration fees amount to 200 francs on the first 100,000 francs of capital, and further 50 francs on each further 100,000 francs or fraction thereof. Added to this are sundry amounts for stamp duty and the costs of certification.

The taxes normally paid by a corporation are the capital tax and the earnings tax. The capital tax is charged at the rate of two per thousand on the corporation's capital, including reserves. The rate of earnings tax is found by first expressing the net earnings as a percentage of the capital on which the capital tax is based; this percentage is then divided by two and the result is the percentage rate of earnings tax but subject to a minimum of 5 per cent and a maximum of 12 per cent.

Holding companies and domiciliary companies are exempt from earnings tax. The holding company is an organization whose objects consist mainly in the administration of holdings and of other business organizations. The domiciliary company is an organization which is domiciled in Liechtenstein, where it may have commercial offices, but which operates mainly abroad. Holding and domiciliary companies merely pay capital tax at the rate of one per thousand of the paid-up capital or of the invested units and reserves, the minimum being 600 francs per annum.

All corporations must pay 3 per cent coupon tax on the dividends distributed. The accounts of this tax must be set out on a special form, which must be submitted each year to the tax administration together with the balance sheet and the profit and loss account.

The Foundation

The creation of a family foundation is a way of settling or endowing property for some specified purpose, notably provision for the cost of educating, equipping or supporting members of one or several families, the pursuance of this purpose being entrusted to a specially authorized body, the board. The board normally achieves this object by making grants out of the revenue of the foundation property or out of the property itself, or both.

The law speaks of a simple family foundation when the foundation property is permanently settled for the purpose of providing for the cost of educating or supporting family members or when it is to be administered and used for similar purposes. A mixed family foundation is one where family members are not the only beneficiaries, but where the settled property or its revenue is to be partially or additionally allocated to purposes outside the family.

The first essential of a family foundation is the foundation property which, either alone or together with its revenue, is to be used for the benefit of the members of one or several specified families. This settlement of property must be of a permanent nature; it cannot simply be a donation or a legacy, *etc.* This property, settled for a permanent purpose, legally constitutes a separate entity in the form of a foundation, *i.e.* it has corporate status. Accordingly, it must by law have a name of its own, a specified purpose and object, and an internal organization. In the case of the family foundation, the corporate status does not depend on registration, *i.e.* registration itself has no constitutive effect.

The settlor, who may be an individual or a corporation or a partnership, is the party who, for the purpose of achieving some specific object, vests certain rights or property in a foundation, so that this property or the revenue thereof may be paid out to the beneficiaries appointed either by name or by class by a particular body appointed for the purpose. The settlor gives the foundation its constitution, specifies the form of the administration and the benefits, and appoints the beneficiaries by name or by class. Subject to certain statutory restrictions, he is free to retain and confer powers and generally to arrange the foundation as he pleases. He may specify the organization in detail or simply in outline. Thus, when setting up the foundation, he may provide that after his death the power to determine the organization devolves upon a third party or on the court or on the Liechtenstein Government.

The governing bodies of the foundation are only vested with those powers which are conferred by the law and, in particular, by the terms of settlement. It is the function of the board to represent the foundation, administer the foundation property, and hand over the benefits to the beneficiaries. If the terms of settlement so provide, the board may also have the power to appoint the beneficiaries. However, the settlor may confer this power upon a special body, the collators, who then appoint the beneficiaries and thereupon instruct the board to allocate the specified benefits to those beneficiaries. If the terms of settlement merely charge the collators to appoint the beneficiaries, but fail to specify the form and amount of the benefits, the board is at liberty to determine the form and amount of the benefits to the beneficiaries appointed by the collators; in case of doubt, the benefits are to be allocated equally *per capita* or *per stirpes* or by groups, unless the terms of settlement provide otherwise.

The auditing body, if provided for by the terms of settlement, must verify the correctness of the board's management, the performance of the foundation's objects, and the allocation of the correct benefits to the beneficiaries specified by the terms of settlement or appointed by the collators or the board.

The beneficiaries are those individuals or organizations to whom benefits are to be awarded out of the foundation. An enforceable claim to such benefits only arises in so far as the settlement or a resolution of the collators or the board grants and awards a beneficial right. The beneficial right may be made subject to certain conditions or events, or it may be irrevocable, or it may lapse on the occurrence of certain events. Needless to say, the beneficial right expires once the settled property has in due course been used up or once the foundation is dissolved. A beneficial right gratuitously conferred will, if the terms of settlement so provide, be beyond the reach of creditors of his beneficiary in proceedings of execution or bankruptcy.

The beneficiaries have no greater and no other claim to benefits than that laid down in the terms of settlement or by the body authorized. The terms of settlement may also provide that any beneficiary challenging the amount or form of the benefits or attacking them to the detriment of other beneficiaries will forfeit his gratuitous beneficial privilege. However, the beneficiary always has the right to demand payment of his benefits in the full amount and in the form provided for by the terms of settlement.

Duty and tax

The endowment of a foundation with rights or property is, for taxation purposes, treated as a donation. Accordingly, under Liechtenstein law, the settlor must pay donation tax, provided that he comes under the tax dominion of Liechtenstein. Endowments which serve the public weal and have no profit-making purpose are exempt from donation tax.

The rate of taxation on the endowment ranges from one-half to 18 per cent; the rate applied in any particular case is that which would apply in the case of estate tax on succession. Thus, for a settlor resident in Liechtenstein, the endowment of a foundation serving family security purposes will be taxed as a donation at the rate of one-half per cent.

Except for public charitable foundations, which are exempt from taxation, it is necessary at the creation of the foundation to pay an initial duty of 2 per thousand of the foundation capital, though not less than 100 francs. Should the foundation carry on business and transactions of commercial nature the registration in the Commercial Register is compulsory and the constitution fee is 2 per cent of the foundation's capital, but for a foundation which does not carry on any trade the constitution fee is reduced to 2 per thousand.

The annual tax payable on the foundation is one per thousand of the foundation capital and reserves, though not less than 600 francs is payable in advance.

If capital and reserves exceed 2,000,000 francs the tax for the excess is reduced to 0·75 per thousand and for amounts over 10,000,000 francs, the rate of 0·50 per thousand is applied.

The Trust

To complete the Liechtenstein P.G.R. code (*Personen- und Gesellschaftsrecht*), particularly the section dealing with the trusteeship (Art. 897 to 932), a new form of enterprise "The Trust Enterprise" was created by the law of 10th April, 1928 (Art. 932a/1 to 170).

(*a*) *Trusteeship*

If the trust is established in writing between the settlor and the trustee, such relation *may* be reported for registration in the Public Register. However, registration of such trust has no constitutive effect: the law expressly provides that the failure to report the trust for registration in the Public Register does not invalidate it; parties who want to keep the trust secret will therefore not register it.

The trust property (also called trust estate, trust fund or principal) consists of all the assets intended for the trust estate by the settlor, regardless of whether such assets are indicated in a general manner only or listed individually in a schedule or an inventory. Finally, anything to be considered as a compensation for the destruction, damage or deprivation of an object belonging to the trust estate, as well as all that is acquired by means of the trust assets themselves or through a legal transaction by means of the trust estate are also part of the trust property (dividends on shares, etc.).

The creditors of the trust property, in the case of a secret trust, may always hold the trustee liable for the debts of the trust estate incurred by him on account of such estate. If the trust deed does not exclude it, the trustee will in certain circumstances also have a right of recourse against the settlor and also against the beneficiary or beneficiaries.

It is immaterial whether the trustee is an individual, a firm or a juridical person. A trustee receives the trust property (capital, asset or right) in order to hold and manage it in his own name. The trustee is nominated by the settlor, by means of an agreement or a trust deed or a last will and testament. The trustee has a legal claim to the reimbursement of all the necessary expenses incurred by him as a result of the acceptance of the trust and spent in the interest of the trust. He has also a claim for compensation of damages accruing to him from the trust property. Contrary to the English law, the trustee is also entitled to a trust salary as an appropriate remuneration for his activity, unless otherwise provided by the trust deed. These claims of the trustee are not legally directed against the trust property, but first of all against the settlor and then against the beneficiaries who are entitled to an interest in the trust property or to the proceeds thereof. Claims may only be made directly against the trust property in the case of an open trust.

(*b*) *Trust Enterprise*

A trust enterprise is an undertaking managed and directed by one or more trustees acting as fiduciary owners thereof. It is nevertheless independent of the trustees: it has assets of its own and bears its own liabilities.

A real trust enterprise has no juridical personality; but it is possible to establish a "figurative" trust enterprise, which is a separate entity in law. The settlor himself may choose between the two possible forms. But the trust enterprise with juridical personality should always be chosen if such undertaking is to pursue economic objectives. In that case it must also be registered in the Commercial Register, and the registered trust enterprise must mention in its name the fact that it is entered in the Commercial Register (*e.g.* registered trust enterprise or registered trust or the like).

A trust enterprise is formed by drawing up the appropriate trust terms, *i.e.* by a deed of constitution or by the trust articles, by means of which the establishment of such an undertaking is declared. The registration with the Commercial Register has no constitutive effect, but is obligatory for a trust enterprise which is to carry on activities of a commercial nature.

A written trust statement is required for constituting a trust enterprise. It must contain the name, head office, duration, objects and purpose of the undertaking and the express indication that it is a trust enterprise. It is essential to mention in the trust articles a reference concerning the amount and nature of the trust fund, and the various items thereof must be listed separately. As regards the organization, it is necessary to indicate the number of trustees, the method of their appointment and possibly of their future substitution.

The enterprise may be established for any freely chosen, well defined and possible objects which are not inconsistent with the public interest, particularly to invest capital, distribute profits, amalgamate undertakings, assign beneficial shares for family welfare, public benefit, charitable or other personal or impersonal purposes; in short, the objects may cover purely economic or purely personal and family aims. Thus the whole trust enterprise may be organized and built up by virtue of its objects along the lines of the family foundation (family trust), or of a commercial enterprise (business trust) or along the lines of a financial or holding company of any kind. The objects and purposes of the enterprise determines the nature of the undertaking.

It is evident that the trust enterprise must be provided with a capital, and such capital may consist of material or immaterial assets, cash, securities, credits, rights or of any property whatsoever. Such trust property includes all the assets which the settlor has destined for such purpose.

The trust articles govern and rule the investment of the trust estate. The law leaves the investment of assets to the discretion of the trustees, but the trust articles may make specific provisions for investment and restrict the discretion otherwise conferred on the trustees.

All the expenses resulting from the constitution and termination of a trust enterprise, such as the salary of the trustee and other allowances for activities under the law or the trust articles, are to be defrayed out of the yield of the trust estate if there are no other provisions to contrary effect in the articles.

The obligations of the trust enterprise towards third parties are solely guaranteed by the trust fund set forth in the trust articles and by the other assets of the trust enterprise. There is no personal liability on the part of those concerned, except for certain obligations of the trust enterprise which are concurrently obligations of all or some of the participants. Needless to say, any participant is of course liable for unauthorized acts or forbearances.

Trust enterprises in Liechtenstein are affected by tax the same way and with the same amounts as the establishment.

LUXEMBOURG

FIDUCIAIRE GENERALE DE LUXEMBOURG

The Grand Duchy of Luxembourg is bounded on the north and west by Belgium, on the south by France and on the east by Germany. The total area is 2,586 square miles with maximum distances of 51 miles from north to south and 35 miles from east to west. The climate is transitional between the maritime type and the semi-continental type.

Total population (1970) is 340,000 of which 78,000 live in Luxembourg-City. The active population is roughly 140,000, of whom 16,000 are in agriculture, 64,000 in industry and 60,000 in services. National income per capita (1969) is U.S.$1,930.

The steel industry, in the southern part of the country, had an output of 5·5 million tons of steel in 1969 and continues to be the backbone of the local economy. Since the early sixties, the Government has made considerable efforts directed towards a wider diversification of industrial activities.

Luxembourg is not a tax haven in the generally accepted meaning of the expression. However, it follows a liberal fiscal policy inasmuch as the activities of pure holding companies are concerned. The activities allowed to such holding companies are strictly defined by law and by the competent administration, and trespassing is penalized by submitting the defaulting company to the common tax system. The justification of this liberal fiscal policy applied to holding companies stems from principles of fiscal justice and from economic grounds.

Communications

The country has excellent communications with the surrounding countries through the state-owned railway system with a total track length of 205 miles. It is served by a good system of roads (3,100 miles) connecting all the principal centres. Air traffic is rapidly increasing and there are daily communications with the major European centres as well as with London and New York. The canalization of the Moselle

River was completed in 1965 and links the Grand Duchy to the main seaports of the Atlantic Coast.

The postal, telephone and telegram system are owned and operated by the Government.

Government

The country is a constitutional monarchy with a hereditary sovereign. The constitution was proclaimed in 1868 and has been modified several times since. Sovereignty is vested in the people who elect a chamber of deputies of 56 members at intervals of five years. The chamber can initiate legislation and amend draft measures, all decisions being taken by a majority vote. The ruler, Grand Duke Jean of Luxembourg, exercises executive power through a ministerial council. The latter is the governing body responsible to the chamber of deputies.

One of the most remarkable features of the Grand Duchy of Luxembourg is its political and economical stability. For many years, the Christian Socialist Party (21 deputies in 1969 elections) has been the leading party in the formation of Governments.

The Grand Duchy of Luxembourg is a member of the following international organizations:

Union Economique Belgo-Luxembourgeoise (Economic Union Treaty between Belgium and Luxembourg);
Benelux (economic treaty between Belgium, the Netherlands and Luxembourg);
European Economic Community (E.E.C.);
European Iron and Steel Community.

Law

Civil law is based on the Code Napoléon and commercial legislation is based on that of Belgium. Its administration is centralized in the minister of justice.

Language

The use of the English language is very widespread with professionals. Besides, everybody speaks and writes German and, to a lesser degree, French.

Currency and Exchange Control

The monetary unit of the Grand Duchy of Luxembourg is the Luxembourg franc, at par with the Belgian franc, one of the most stable currencies in the world. Both currencies are legal tender in Luxembourg. There are no restrictions on transfers of capital and income.

Financial and Professional Services

The country enjoys very large facilities as regards the availability of lawyers, accountants and banks. The banks also act as stockbrokers and investment advisers.

Internal Tax Structure

During World War II, German tax law was introduced in the Grand Duchy of Luxembourg, then under German occupation. After the end of the war in 1944, the German legislation remained in force until the vote of a new income tax law in December 1967. This law is generally applicable since 1st January, 1969. It is drawn up in French and amalgamates a great number of the previous German executory decrees.

The common tax law of Luxembourg is based upon the taxability of the world-wide income and assets of national residents and the taxability of certain income from Luxembourg sources or derived from a permanent establishment in Luxembourg of non-residents, as well as certain of their assets located in Luxembourg. Transactions executed and services rendered on the territory of the Grand Duchy are subject to the value added tax (T.V.A.) at rates varying from 2 to 10 per cent.

The Holding Company

On 31st July, 1929, the chamber of deputies voted a special law applicable to "holding companies". These companies are not subject to any direct or indirect taxation; the common tax law briefly outlined above is not applicable to them. Instead, they only have to pay a minor yearly composition duty of 0·16 per cent which is calculated on the value of their issued shares and debentures. The minimum yearly tax is L.F.1,500.

However, the activities of holding companies are limited: they may participate in any form whatsoever in other domestic or foreign enterprises or may engage in the administration and the realization of such participating interests but they may not have any direct industrial activity or maintain any commercial establishment open to the public. They may own all kinds of shares (except shares of limited partnerships or private partnerships), bonds or debentures, and in connection with such securities any patent rights or licences. In the administration and management of these portfolios, they may grant loans and advances to the companies in which they have an interest, or to their licensees.

The holding company may finance its activities through its share capital, reserves, undistributed profits, bank overdrafts or advances received from its shareholders. However, in normal cases, its loan capital may not exceed three times the share capital.

In detail, the income statement of a Luxembourg holding company could comprise the following items:

Income

Dividends received;
Interest received from advances, loans, bonds and debentures;
realized gains on the sale of securities;
patent royalties received;
realized gains on the sale of patent rights.

Expenses

interest paid for advances, loans;
general administrative expenses, such as remuneration, fees and office expenses;
losses suffered on the sale of securities and patent rights.

Luxembourg holding companies may not own directly any real estate, except for the accommodation of their own offices.

Income received by a holding company is not subject to any taxation in the hands of the company itself. Furthermore, dividends and interest paid by the company are not subject to any withholding tax and are paid out gross. However, holding companies may not claim credit for withholding taxes suffered on dividend, interest or patent royalty income received by them, be it from national or foreign sources, since, in general, they are excluded from the provisions of tax treaties.

Laws for all corporate entities, including holding companies, were enacted in 1915. Any form of commercial or civil entity may qualify as a holding company. However, since almost all holding companies have been incorporated in the form of a joint stock company, the following comments may be made on the corporate legislation applicable to this company form.

Joint stock companies are organized according to the terms of articles of incorporation. These have to be sworn before a notary public and must be published in full in the official journal (*Mémorial*). The company must always have at least seven shareholders; their nationality is irrelevant. It must maintain registered offices in the Grand Duchy of Luxembourg. The general meeting of shareholders is the supreme authority of the company and has to appoint at least three directors and one statutory auditor; their nationality is irrelevant. The directors are in charge of the day-to-day management of the company. The auditor has to control the operations of the company and give an opinion on the yearly financial statements which have to be published in a condensed form in the official journal.

The share capital of the company may be expressed in local or foreign currency and is divided into bearer or registered shares which have the same value and the same voting rights. Besides the shares which are issued against capital, it is permitted to issue beneficiary shares to which certain rights may be attached (voting right, dividend right, right to winding-up proceeds). The whole share capital has to be subscribed at the time of incorporation and each share must be paid up to the extent of 20 per cent at least. The board of directors decides when and how the unpaid portions of the share capital are called for payment. As long, however, as the shares are not fully paid up, they have to remain registered shares and their transfer is subject to the authorization of the board of directors. The transfer of registered shares is operated by inscription in the share register which has to be kept at the registered offices of the company. The transfer of bearer shares is operated by simple transmission of the documents. Every director and every statutory auditor has to deposit at least one share of the company as a guarantee for the execution of his duties.

The formation of a holding company in the form of a joint stock company usually takes a very short time. The incorporation cost comprises the following items:

(*a*) a single capital contribution duty of 0·5 per cent which is calculated on the total issued share capital, whether fully paid up or not. The same duty is due on the occasion of any capital increase. From 1st January, 1973, the capital contribution duty will be one per cent;
(*b*) the cost of registration of the company at the Register of Firms. This fee is payable once only, and amounts to L.F.1,600 for companies having a share capital exceeding L.F.1,000,000;
(*c*) the cost of publication of the articles of incorporation in the official journal. Normally this cost amounts to approximately L.F.6,000;
(*d*) the fees of the notary public executing the deed of incorporation vary according to the amount of share capital involved;
(*e*) the fees of accountants, lawyers and notaries consulted upon incorporation vary according to the time spent and the responsibilities undertaken.

The statutory requirements which a holding company must comply with are:

(*a*) filing of quarterly returns for the composition duty of 0·16 per cent;
(*b*) holding of the annual meeting in Luxembourg: the shareholders may be present or represented by proxies;
(*c*) maintenance of its accounts (and of the corporate registers) in the registered offices in Luxembourg;
(*d*) publication of the yearly financial statements (balance sheet and income statement) in a condensed form in the official journal.

The annual maintenance cost comprises the following items:

(*a*) composition duty of 0·16 per cent calculated on the value of the issued shares and bonds;
(*b*) cost of publication of the financial statements, usually L.F.1,500;
(*c*) cost of calling the annual meeting (in case of bearer shares) by two consecutive advertisements in one local newspaper and in the official journal, usually L.F.2,500;
(*d*) fees for domiciliation and services performed by lawyers, accountants and local directors if applicable: these fees vary according to the time spent and the responsibilities undertaken.

The structure of the Luxembourg holding company has been used for the following purposes:

investment companies (in conjunction with repurchase companies and advisory companies);

management trusts;

management companies of mutual investment funds: holding companies, which must have a paid-in capital of L.F.5,000,000 at least, have been allowed to manage a portfolio of securities not owned by themselves and to issue certificates representing a fraction of this portfolio;

finance companies: under certain conditions, holding companies have been allowed to grant advances to companies of the same group in which they do not have any direct interest and to finance these advances through bond issues not exceeding ten times their share capital.

NETHERLANDS ANTILLES

CURAÇAO INTERNATIONAL TRUST COMPANY N.V.

The Netherlands Antilles consist of two groups of three islands each: the Windward Islands—Saba, St. Eustatius and St. Maarten (about half of the latter island belongs to France)—which are situated some forty miles to the east of Puerto Rico, and the Leeward Islands—Aruba, Curaçao and Bonaire—which are to be found about six hundred miles to the south-west. Curaçao, the largest of the islands, lies about 40 miles off the Venezuelan coast at about 12° 15′ north latitude.

Despite their tropical location, all the six islands enjoy a pleasant climate by virtue of the almost continuous north-east Trade Winds. The average temperature is 82°F. (27·5°C.). August and September are the hottest months (87·5F. at noon), whereas January and February are the coolest (around 81°F. at noon).

Rainfall on the Leeward Islands is light (around 20 inches or 50 cm. per annum), occurring in two short rainy seasons. Although the rainfall on the Windwards is about twice that on the Leewards, the average temperatures are about the same on all the six islands.

The average humidity is about 75 per cent.

The total area is about 393 square miles (= 1·018 km^2).

As of 1st January, 1972 the total population was 223,550, divided over the island as follows:

Island	*Area in s.m.*	*Population*
Saba	5	750
St. Eustatius	12	1,300
St. Maarten	16	7,500
Aruba	70	61,000
Curaçao	180	145,000
Bonaire	110	8,000
TOTAL	393	223,550

Communications

Its favourable location has made the Netherlands Antilles, in particular the islands Curaçao and Aruba, a very important traffic junction between Europe, North America and South America; many shipping companies and airlines have included the Netherlands Antilles in their schedules and use Aruba and Curaçao as a bunkering station. There are large oil refineries in Curaçao (Shell Oil) and Aruba (Standard Oil N.J.). The Free Zones which have been created in Aruba and in Curaçao, have their share in the increased volume of transportation. The association of the Netherlands Antilles with the E.E.C. has also proven to be of great importance.

Air and mail connections with the rest of the world are excellent. The same is true as regards telegraphic (state owned and I.T.T.) services, telex and telephone.

The interinsular connections (mainly by air) and communications are very good.

Government

The Netherlands Antilles is one of the three partners of the Kingdom of the Netherlands. The other two are the Netherlands and Surinam. The Netherlands Antilles, like each of the other two partners is fully autonomous in its internal affairs.

The form of government is a parliamentary democracy. There is general suffrage for men and women alike.

Matters of common interest to the partners, notably foreign policy and defence, are handled by the Parliament of the Kingdom (consisting of the Upper and Lower Houses of the Netherlands, supplemented by members of the Parliament of the other partners) and by the Council of Ministers of the Kingdom (consisting of the Cabinet Ministers of the Netherlands and the accredited plenipotentiary Ministers from the other partners).

The Government of the Netherlands Antilles consists of a Governor (as the Queen's representative) and a Council of Ministers. The latter is responsible to the Parliament (*Staten*) of the Netherlands Antilles.

The Netherlands Antilles is divided into four (municipal) island territories, to wit: Aruba, Curaçao, Bonaire and the Windward Islands.

The representative body is the Island Council, which has the right to enact laws governing municipal affairs. The Council is presided over by a Lieutenant Governor (*Gezaghebber*), who is appointed by the Queen. The day-to-day administration and the enforcement of the municipal laws are in the hands of the Administrative Board (*Bestuurscollege*), consisting of the Lieutenant Governor and several members of the Island Council.

The Netherlands Antilles enjoy a political stability and social peace.

Law

The Netherlands Antilles has adopted the civil law system. Its laws are, with a few exceptions, based on the same principles as those in force in the Netherlands.

Language

Most residents are multilingual. The languages most commonly known are Papiamentu, Dutch, English and Spanish.

Currency and Exchange Control

The currency is the Netherlands Antilles guilder (N.A.f.) which (in 1972) is equivalent to U.S.$0·56. As a rule all transactions between non-residents and residents of the Netherlands Antilles involving currencies, gold, claims on and other indebtedness of residents, real estate and movable property situated in the Netherlands Antilles, are subject to the approval of the Foreign Exchange Control Board. The same is true for the acquisition, importation and exportation by non-residents, of such valuables. (Foreign Exchange Ordinance 1940.)

On certain conditions investment companies, patent holding companies and other Netherlands Antilles corporations not actively engaged in local trade or business, and formed by and for the account of non-residents with foreign capital, can obtain a general licence to freely dispose of their capital and profits as far as such capital and profits are derived from foreign sources.

FINANCIAL AND PROFESSIONAL SERVICES

There are several well qualified civil law notaries, law offices and public auditor's firms in the Netherlands Antilles. There are no stock brokers. Investment advisory services are supplied by the local banks.

There are various banking institutions in the Netherlands Antilles which are well known in most other countries. They offer all kinds of local and international banking services.

In addition, there are various trust companies, several of which are subsidiaries of a bank.

INTERNAL TAX STRUCTURE

Profits Tax

Limited liability companies (U.S. "corporations") incorporated under the laws of the Netherlands Antilles, are subject to a corporate income tax (profits tax) on their aggregate global net profits on an annual basis, irrespective of the country wherefrom the corporation derives the relative income. The standard rate of this tax is between 27 per cent and 34 per cent (sliding scale) depending on the amount of the income. In addition, there is a municipal surtax of 15 per cent of the tax amount. However, there are exceptions and the following classes of corporations qualify for a preferential tax treatment:

(*a*) *Investment and holding companies*

Under the provisions of Article 14 of the Netherlands Antilles Profit Tax Ordinance 1940, income from securities, which term includes shares, bonds, notes and other interest bearing debts, is subject to tax at the reduced rate of 2·4 per cent on the net profit not exceeding N.A. guilders 100,000 (approx. U.S.$55,000) and 3 per cent on the excess thereof. Capital gains are not subject to tax; on the other hand capital losses are not tax deductible. Interest paid by such corporation is only deductible for N.A. tax purposes if paid to a banking institution. There is no surtax. The tax rates for the above-mentioned income are guaranteed until the last day of the fiscal year started prior to 1st July, 1979. (N.A. Ordinance of 31st August, 1970.)

(b) Patent holding companies

Under the provisions of Article 14A of the Netherlands Antilles Profit Tax Ordinance 1940, royalties and rentals received in respect of copyrights, patents, trademarks, films and industrial, commercial and scientific equipment, real estate, and compensations received for rendering technical assistance outside the Netherlands Antilles are subject to tax at the same rate as mentioned under (*a*) above. There is no surtax. Capital gains on the alienation of rights as mentioned heretofore or of equipment are not subject to tax; capital losses (including depreciation) are not tax deductible. The tax rates are guaranteed until the last day of the fiscal year started prior to 1st July, 1979.

(c) Ocean shipping and aviation companies

Under the provisions of Article 9A of the Netherlands Antilles Profit Tax Ordinance 1940, ocean shipping and aviation companies, under certain conditions will enjoy the following tax advantages:

partial tax exemption resulting in an effective tax rate between 8·69 per cent and 10·95 per cent;
guaranteed maximum of rate of surtax of 15 per cent (this surtax is included in the above-mentioned effective tax rates);
the tax rates will not be affected by any amendment of the Netherlands Antilles tax laws, as far as the profits made in the period *starting* with the first fiscal year which ends after 30th June, 1966, and *ending* with the last fiscal year, which starts prior to 1st July, 1981, are concerned;
discretionary accelerated writing-off is permitted up to one-third of the acquisition costs;
an investment tax credit is allowed for two years, amounting to 8 per cent per annum;
there is a loss carry-over for six subsequent years. (However, there is no carry-back facility);
an amendment of Article 9A within the period described in this section will not affect already existing companies.

A limited liability company wishing to avail itself of the tax facilities for ocean shipping and aviation companies must meet the following requirements:

(1) the company must be formed under Netherlands Antillean law;
(2) it must have its registered office in the Netherlands Antilles;
(3) in so far as the company itself is the carrier, the day-to-day management of business must be conducted in the Netherlands Antilles.

The tax facilities apply primarily to ocean-going ships registered in the Kingdom of the Netherlands. However, ocean-going ships operated by an Antillean limited liability company but not registered in the Kingdom of the Netherlands may—by Antillean Government Decree—be subject to the same regulations as those that are. The profits made with such ships will then be taxed at the special rate. They may be ships sailing under a flag other than the Dutch flag and chartered by an Antillean limited liability company. The special tariff will not apply unless the regulations governing the safety and welfare of the ships' crew in the country of registration are at least as good as those in force in the Netherlands Antilles. In accordance with an Antillean Government Decree promulgated in 1967 (N.A. Government Information Sheet 1967, No. 87), ships registered in the following countries will in any case be held to meet the above-mentioned requirement: Norway, Sweden, Denmark, Finland, Iceland, Federal Republic of Germany, Britain, France, Belgium, Switzerland, Israel and the U.S.A.

(*d*) *Free Zone companies*

Free Zones have been created in Curaçao and Aruba. Goods may be imported, processed, packed and re-exported duty free. N.A. corporations formed to operate in the Free Zone mainly, are subject to a profits tax at a rate of one-third of the standard rates. Profits made by incidental activities directed to the Netherlands Antilles itself, are taxable at the full rates: 27 per cent to 34 per cent (sliding scale), plus 15 per cent surtax. The taxation at one-third of the standard rates is guaranteed until 1st July, 1981.

(*e*) *Financial holding companies*

Netherlands Antilles corporations are used by international companies to float Eurobond issues. The liberal corporation law and foreign exchange controls in the Netherlands Antilles play an important part in this matter. The financial holding companies are taxable at the special rates of 2·4 per cent and 3 per cent with respect to the interest on their income from non-U.S. sources, and at the rates of 24 per cent to 30 per cent with respect to their U.S. source income. (See also the United States–Netherlands Antilles Tax Treaty.)

The interest paid by the corporation to its bondholders is deductible as expense taxwise, and will thus reduce the taxable net income of the corporation on the following conditions:

the bonds should be listed on an official stock exchange; the net taxable income derived from the proceeds of the bond issue of the corporation should not be less than one per cent of the face value of the bond issue; a tax ruling should be obtained for each and every bond issue.

(f) Real estate companies

Under the provisions of Article 12 of the Netherlands Antilles Profit Tax Ordinance 1940, a Netherlands Antilles corporation may own real estate outside the territory of the Netherlands Antilles. If, in the country where the real estate is situated there exists a form of tax on profits derived from such property, the Netherlands Antilles corporation will be taxed in the Netherlands Antilles at rates of 2·4 per cent and 3 per cent as described under (*a*) above, plus the municipal surtax of 15 per cent.

If the corporation has been formed with foreign capital and for account of non-residents of the Netherlands Antilles and in consequence the corporation is exonerated from exchange restrictions, no surtax is due provided that ever since its incorporation all shares are owned by non-residents. If such a company owns real estate in Holland or Surinam, profits from such property will be entirely tax exempt. (See also the United States–Netherlands Antilles Tax Treaty.)

Capital gains on real estate are taxable at the same low rates. Capital losses are deductible for tax purposes. (When a Netherlands Antilles corporation is dissolved and the property is distributed, the capital gain will be determined at the difference between the value of the assets on the date of distribution and their book value.) Depreciation is allowed to a certain extent.

Instead of Article 12, a real estate company could make use of Article 14A of the Netherlands Antilles Profit Tax Ordinance 1940. If the corporation elects to be taxed under the provision of Article 14A, Section 1 (b), its rental income will be taxed at the rates of 2·4 per cent and 3 per cent described under (*a*) above. No surtax is due. Capital gains are tax exempt; on the other hand, capital losses are not deductible for N.A. tax purposes. Depreciation is disallowed. In this case it is not required that in the country where the real estate is situated there exists a tax on profits derived from such property.

(g) Companies with foreign establishment

Under the provisions of Article 12 of the Netherlands Antilles Profit Tax Ordinance of 1940, a Netherlands Antilles corporation which has a permanent establishment of business outside the Netherlands Antilles in a country where there exists a form of tax on the profits of such an establishment, will be taxed in about the same manner as described under (*f*) above.

Capital Tax

Corporations are not subject to a capital or wealth tax.

Withholding Tax

There is no withholding tax on dividends and interest paid by a Netherlands Antilles corporation. Neither is there an income tax on such payments by a Netherlands Antilles corporation to non-residents of the Netherlands Antilles.

Estate Tax

Shares owned by a non-resident are not subject to estate tax or inheritance tax upon his death.

Sales Tax

There is no sales tax (*i.e.* turnover tax or value added tax).

Income Tax

A non-resident managing director (U.S. "director") or director (U.S. "supervisory director") of a Netherlands Antilles corporation is subject to personal income tax on his remunerations as such, on an annual basis. Should such a person have no other income taxable in the Netherlands Antilles, then he would be taxed as follows:

Net income		*Tax* 1972 (married):	
Under N.A.f.3,300			nil
N.A.f.	3,400	N.A.f.	20
"	5,000	"	119
"	10,000	"	593
"	20,000	"	2,388
"	30,000	"	5,206
"	100,000	"	32,993

NOTE: The maximum marginal rate is 44% on income in excess of N.A.f.100,000.

Stamp Tax

Stock certificates and bond certificates: if signed in the Netherlands Antilles, a stamp tax of 4 per mille on the face value of each certificate is due (there is a rounding off of differences). If signed outside the Netherlands Antilles, no such stamp tax is due until the certificates come into circulation in the Netherlands Antilles.

General deeds of agreement: N.A. guilders 2·00 per sheet (double folio).

Commercial Paper: short paper, N.A. guilders 0·10; other paper, N.A. guilders 0·20.

Deeds of indebtedness not being securities or commercial paper: N.A. guilders 0·20 for every N.A. guilders 100.

Special Facilities

Brief mention should be made of the existence of special tax and other facilities for oil companies, insurance companies, hotel business operating in the Netherlands Antilles, for the establishment of new industries and for land development.

Tax Treaties

The Netherlands Antilles has concluded tax treaties with the United States, the United Kingdom, the other two component parts of the Kingdom of the Netherlands (Holland and Surinam) and the Kingdom of Denmark.

United States

Under the terms of the Income Tax Convention between the United States and the Netherlands, as extended to the Netherlands Antilles and subsequently modified by Protocol of 23rd October, 1963 (the Supplementary Convention of 20th December, 1965 between the United States and the Netherlands is not applicable to the Netherlands Antilles), a Netherlands Antilles corporation is subject to 15 per cent U.S. withholding tax on dividends from U.S. sources and is exempt from U.S. withholding tax on interest and royalties, provided that the corporation waives its right to be taxed in the Netherlands Antilles with respect to its U.S. source income at the preferential rates accorded by Articles 13, 14 and 14A of the Netherlands Antilles Profit Tax Ordinance 1940, and at the same time elects to be taxed in the Netherlands Antilles at the rates provided for in Article 8A of the same Ordinance, as regards its U.S. source income.

These rates are:

15 per cent on net dividend income (*i.e.* after U.S. withholding tax and allocable expenses);
24 per cent on net interest and royalty income not exceeding N.A. guilders 100,000 (approx. U.S.$55,000) and 30 per cent on the excess thereof.
There is no surtax.

In order to calculate net taxable income, deductions are allowed for U.S. withholding tax and for allocable expenses.

Gains realized by a Netherlands Antilles corporation on the sale of securities, whether short term or long term, are exempt both from United States and Netherlands Antilles tax.

Under the terms of the treaty, income from real estate situated in the United States and owned by a Netherlands Antilles corporation is subject to U.S. tax only. (See also under (*f*) above.)

Under the treaty provisions, dividends, interest and royalties received by a Netherlands Antilles corporation from a U.S. corporation, 25 per cent or more of the stock whereof is owned by the Netherlands Antilles corporation are, if less than 60 per cent of the U.S. company's gross income consists of "passive income", taxable in the United States at the rate of 15 per cent as far as dividends are concerned, and exempt from U.S. tax, while such income is subject to Netherlands Antilles tax at the special 2·4 per cent and 3 per cent rates.

In case a Netherlands Antilles corporation owns 95 per cent or more of the outstanding stock of a U.S. corporation, dividends paid by the U.S. corporation to the N.A. corporation are subject to 5 per cent U.S. withholding tax, such dividends being subject to Netherlands Antilles tax at the rates of 2·4 per cent and 3 per cent.

Under the treaty provisions, Netherlands Antilles investment companies and patent holding companies which are wholly and solely owned *either* by one or more Dutch corporations *or* by one or more individual residents of the Netherlands or the Netherlands Antilles will enjoy the preferential withholding tax rates in the United States of 15 per cent on U.S. source dividends and nil on U.S. source interest and royalties, while being subject to the low 2·4 per cent and 3 per cent Netherlands Antilles tax rate on that income.

Dividends received from a Netherlands Antilles corporation by its shareholders who are neither U.S. citizens nor U.S. residents, are not subject to U.S. personal income tax. (In the absence of treaty relief, all dividends paid by a Netherlands Antilles corporation would have been subject to U.S. personal income tax—irrespective of the citizenship or residence of the shareholders—if 50 per cent or more of the gross income of the corporation over the 3-year period ending with the close of its taxable year preceding the declaration of the dividends, was effectively connected with the conduct of a trade or business within the United States.)

United Kingdom

Under the terms of the Income Tax Convention between the United States and the Netherlands, dated 31st October, 1967, as extended to the Netherlands Antilles, effective 1st January, 1970, a Netherlands Antilles corporation is subject to 15 per cent U.K. withholding tax on dividends from U.K. sources and is exempt from U.K. withholding tax on interest and royalties from U.K. sources, provided that the corporation waives its right to be taxed in the Netherlands Antilles with respect to its U.K. source income at the preferential rates accorded by Articles 13, 14 and 14A of the Netherlands Antilles Profit Tax Ordinance 1940 and at the same time elects to be taxed in the Netherlands Antilles at the rates provided for in Article 8A of the same Ordinance as regards its income from U.K. sources. (For descriptions of the tax rates under said Article 8A see above under United States.)

In order to calculate net taxable income, deductions are allowed for U.K. withholding tax and for allocable expenses.

Gains realized by a Netherlands Antilles corporation on the sale of securities, whether short term or long term, are exempt both from U.K. and N.A. tax.

Holland and Surinam

The arrangement between Holland, Surinam and the Netherlands Antilles (which three countries form the Kingdom of the Netherlands) with respect to the avoidance of double taxation, is part of the General Law of 28th October, 1964 (Stb. 425) of the Kingdom.

Under the terms of the said law, dividends received by a Netherlands Antilles corporation from Dutch sources are subject to Dutch withholding tax at the rate of 15 per cent rather than at the standard rate of 25 per cent. Where the Netherlands Antilles corporation owns 25 per cent or more of the outstanding stock of the Dutch corporation, dividends received from the latter corporation are totally exempt from Dutch withholding tax. There is no Dutch withholding tax on interest or royalties. Gains on the sale of securities are exempt from Dutch tax by virtue of the Dutch Corporate Tax Law, provided that the Netherlands Antilles corporation is not engaged in trade or business in Holland through a permanent establishment or permanent representative.

The arrangement between the Netherlands Antilles and Surinam is to be found in the same law and is almost of the same nature as that between the Netherlands Antilles and Holland.

Denmark

Under the terms of the Income Tax Convention between Denmark and the Netherlands, dated 20th February, 1957 as amended by Supplementary Convention of 20th January, 1966 and as extended to the Netherlands Antilles, dividends received by a Netherlands Antilles corporation from Danish sources are subject to Danish withholding tax at the rate of 15 per cent rather than at the standard rate of 30 per cent. Where the Netherlands Antilles corporation owns 25 per cent or more of the outstanding stock of the Danish corporation, dividends are exempt from Danish withholding tax. There is no Danish withholding tax on interest or royalties. Gains on the sale of securities are exempt from Danish tax.

Available Entities

The tax benefits described above are in general only available to a limited liability company ("corporation") incorporated under the laws of the Netherlands Antilles, called a "*Naamloze Vennootschap*" or (abbreviated) "N.V.".

The Company

Such a corporation is formed under a deed of incorporation drawn up before a notary public in the Netherlands Antilles. The deed of incorporation which contains the articles of incorporation of the company is subject to the approval of the Minister of Justice. The incorporation usually takes several weeks.

The corporation may have nominative or bearer shares, or both types. There are no restrictions with respect to the number of shareholders: the corporation may have one shareholder only.

The corporation may repurchase its own shares. The shares repurchased will lose the voting rights and the right to dividends declared while in portfolio. Managing directors and directors need not be shareholders. Annually a shareholders' meeting should be held in the Netherlands Antilles. At this meeting the annual report and the financial statements will be discussed and determined. Since a meeting may be held by proxy, there is no need for directors and shareholders to be present personally. The corporation must (annually) file a Netherlands Antilles profit tax return within six months after the close of each fiscal year mentioned in its articles of incorporation. Such return must be accompanied by financial statements and supporting papers. It is not required that the corporation's books be kept in the Netherlands Antilles but the inspector may require them to be presented for inspection.

The costs of incorporation of a Netherlands Antilles corporation consists of notarial charges (which are based on the amount of authorized capital), of stamp taxes on the Ministerial Decree, of costs of publication of the deed of incorporation in the Official Gazette, and of the registration fee of the Commercial Register (which is based upon the amount of paid-up capital).

The notarial charges are:

For a corporation with an authorized capital:
- not exceeding N.A.f.50,000: N.A.f.530
- between N.A.f.50,000 and N.A.f.100,000:
  - N.A.f.530 plus 4¼ per cent over N.A.f.50,000
- between N.A.f.100,000 and N.A.f.200,000:
  - N.A.f.750 plus 2½ per cent on excess over N.A.f.100,000
- between N.A.f.200,000 and N.A.f.1,000,000:
  - N.A.f.1,000 plus 1¼ per cent on excess over N.A.f.200,000

over N.A.f.1,000,000:
N.A.f.2,000 plus N.A.f.500 for each additional N.A.f.1,000,000.

The stamp tax on the Ministerial Decree amounts to N.A.f.100.
Publication costs amount to approximately N.A.f.100.
The registration fees of the Commercial Register are:

For a corporation with a paid capital:	N.A.f.
not exceeding N.A.f.5,000	10
between N.A.f.5,000 and N.A.f.10,000	15
over N.A.f. 10,000 up to N.A.f. 25,000	20
over N.A.f. 25,000 up to N.A.f. 50,000	50
over N.A.f. 50,000 up to N.A.f. 100,000	100
over N.A.f. 100,000 up to N.A.f. 200,000	150
over N.A.f. 200,000 up to N.A.f. 500,000	250
over N.A.f. 500,000 up to N.A.f.1,000,000	500
over N.A.f.1,000,000	1,000

THE NEW HEBRIDES

INVESTORS TRUST LIMITED

The New Hebrides, a group of about eighty habitable but undeveloped islands comprising 5,700 square miles, lie in a 600-mile chain between Fiji and the north-eastern coast of Australia.

The climate is subtropical and, as in all South Pacific islands, is freshened by the South-east Trades which are a permanent feature from April through to December. The rainfall is mainly confined to a four-month wet season, but there is sufficient precipitation during the remainder of the year to maintain luxuriant vegetation.

Commercial activity is largely confined to Vila (called Port Vila by the French) on the central island of Efate, where both the British and the French maintain substantial residences. The up-to-date "Condominium Building", housing jointly controlled services, is a prominent feature of the waterfront main street, bearing the appropriate name of "Rue Higginson". The only other town in the group is Luganville, commonly called Santo, on the northern island of Espiritu Santo.

Communications

Jet access is available by U.T.A.'s daily fifty-five minute flight from New Caledonia. Fiji Airways, presently serving the area with jet-prop Hawker Siddeleys, will be flying B.A.C. 111s on the 500-mile trip from Nandi Airport within the next few months. Both New Caledonia and Fiji constitute major links in the world's jet services.

An appropriation for telex has been included in the current Condominium budget. The present cable and telephone services are efficient, but the latter is available for part of the day only, and will need extension shortly. A letter to the United States takes two to three days; Europe, two to four days; Australian and New Zealand mail often involves only twenty-four hours.

Government

The New Hebrides is the world's last effective Condominium, being ruled jointly by Britain and France under a treaty known as "The Protocol" of 1914, under which each metropolitan power retains jurisdiction over its own nationals and over those, who on taking up residence, opt for its protection.

The native people, who number about 70,000 out of a total population of about 80,000, have no political awareness and, because they are scattered across 100,000 square miles of the Pacific Ocean, there is no common language among them.

Law

Because of the unique constitutional structure, companies may use both British and French law. In each case, all laws of general application in those countries apply in the group; both have been modified and, in the case of British Law, special local enactments provide specific tax haven facilities.

Language

English is spoken in all commercial establishments and government agencies, and is understood everywhere. The natives speak pidgin English (called Bichelamar by the French), but are not involved to any significant extent in commerce.

Currency and Exchange Control

The group is outside the sterling area, the officially recognized currencies being the New Hebridean franc (entirely unconnected with the French Pacific franc) and the Australian dollar. One hundred francs is equivalent to one Australian dollar. There are no exchange controls, and banks can hold accounts in any currency.

Financial and Professional Services

Commercial facilities have expanded over the last year. Substantial New Zealand and Australian legal and accounting firms are represented. Banking facilities are provided in modern branches of French, Australian and English Banks which offer savings account facilities at 4 per cent and fixed deposit at rates between 4·5 per cent and 5·5 per cent. Four trust companies, Investors' Trust Ltd., Melanesia International Trust Co. Ltd., Burns Philp & International Trust Co. Ltd., and New Hebrides Trust Co. Ltd. provide trustee, nominee and management services to outsiders.

Internal Tax Structure

The only levies made by the authorities are import and export duties at a nominal rate, business licence fees and document (stamp) duties. Business licence fees apply only to local businesses, but stamp duties are levied on documents having effect in the group. Secrecy provisions protect local information that is disclosed. The rates of duty run from 0·2 per cent for the transfer of marketable securities (shares, *etc.*) to 3·5 per cent for land. There are no other taxes, duties, or levies of any sort. No guarantees are offered, but because the protocol requires that all citizens shall enjoy equal rights of trade, neither power may tax without agreement from the other. The balance between the two powers and the nature of the existing social and economic structure makes change unlikely.

Tax Treaties

There are no tax treaties, and it is believed none are contemplated.

Available Entities

Under the dual legal system, it is possible to form almost any entity or combination of entities that can be imagined, but because the tax haven development is, at the moment, mainly British, the popular structures are companies and trusts. The recently enacted Companies Regulation is based on the United Kingdom Companies Act 1948 but contains some provisions from the United Kingdom Companies Act 1967 and the Bahamas Regulation. Registration fees are one-twentieth of 1 per cent of the registered capital, with a minimum of $200. The annual licence fee is calculated in exactly the same way. No-par shares are possible but only in unlimited companies.

Company formation is by permit. The application must disclose beneficial ownership, but its contents are protected. A permit is discretionary but is granted automatically in a standard offshore operation for companies of good standing. There are no restrictions on the business of local companies, but only non-local companies may utilize the secrecy provisions of the Regulation. They may do only such local business as is in furtherance of their offshore activities. Formation ordinarily takes about two weeks. There are no restrictions on the nationality of shareholders or directors. A local registered office must be maintained, audited annual balance sheets (protected by the secrecy provisions) must be filed, and at least one directors' meeting must be held in the New Hebrides each year. Private companies, which in essence are those not offering shares publicly, may pass resolutions by signed entry in the company's minute book.

The standard minimum cost of incorporation is about $900. Maintenance, *i.e.* provisions of shareholders and directors, holding statutory meetings, filing returns and audited balance sheets, costs about $550 a year, exclusive of accountancy costs. Fees are negotiable for management.

The commonest transactions involve back-to-back companies and trusts of a passive nature. Many transactions are being arranged by international financiers which revolve around the savings that are effected by the payment of withholding tax only. At the moment, there are relatively few companies producing an active income, but it is clear that a large number of international sales organizations will be represented in the group in the near future.

NORFOLK ISLAND

PERMANENT TRUSTEE COMPANY OF NORFOLK ISLAND LIMITED

Norfolk Island is a small island of volcanic origin situated approximately 1,000 miles north-east of Sydney, Australia and about 800 miles east of the Australian coastline. It was discovered by Captain Cook in 1774 during his second voyage of discovery to the South Seas. At the time of its discovery it was completely uninhabited and there are no native or indigenous people. It enjoys an almost perfect climate, and as it is scenically one of the most beautiful islands in the world, it is fast becoming an important tourist centre. The Island contains some 8,500 acres and is approximately 5 miles long and 3 miles wide. The centre of the Island is dominated by the twin peaks of Mount Pitt and Mount Bates which rise to over 1,000 feet. They are covered by the unique Norfolk Island pines, which are world famous. The population is approximately 1,300 of whom about half were born on the Island, the remainder being born elsewhere mainly in Australia or New Zealand.

Tourism is the main industry but the absence of taxation and other fiscal imposts is leading to the rapid development of the Island as an investment and business centre of international importance.

There are no indigenous people on Norfolk Island and hence there are no racial problems of any kind as the people are homogeneous. The Island has a long and colourful history, having originally been a convict settlement. Many traces of the convict era remain and incidentally add to the Island's attraction as a tourist centre. The last convicts were withdrawn in 1854 and shortly afterwards most of the descendants from the famous "Mutiny on the Bounty" were transferred from Pitcairn Island by the British Government. Many of the islanders can trace their ancestry back to the original participants in the famous mutiny.

The people of Norfolk Island are basically conservative in their outlook and all forms of taxation and government coercion are anathema to them. The economy is sound and rapidly expanding as the tourist trade continues to grow and the commercial turnover increases with the Island's growing importance as a tax haven. The sale of postage stamps (which are much sought after throughout the world) is a major source of the Island's revenue but this is rapidly being augmented by company registration fees which are now in themselves becoming quite a major factor in the Island's economy.

The fortunate combination of a sound economy with political stability seems likely to continue for a considerable time.

Norfolk Island is a unique tax haven in many ways. Its economy is soundly based, and seems certain to continue to improve, as the air service is brought up to date and the telephone installed. It is politically stable and is remote from any of the world's trouble spots. Its currency is the Australian dollar, which is becoming stronger and seems certain to continue to do so, particularly as the value of Australian mineral exports grows in the next decade. It also provides, at reasonable cost, the protection and certainty of a British based legal system. At the present time, Australia is attracting overseas investment from all parts of the western world and, with its own tax haven on its very doorstep, provides a unique possibility for both high income earning and capital gain. Accordingly, whilst Norfolk Island can be of great use to persons wishing to invest in other parts of the world, it is uniquely suitable for overseas investors wishing to take advantage of Australia's prosperity and economic growth.

Communications

Qantas, Australia's international airline, operates a regular air service between Sydney and Norfolk Island and a weekly air service is offered by Air New Zealand between Norfolk Island and Auckland. The frequency of the service between Sydney and the Island depends on the tourist demand and at the moment varies from bi-weekly to daily. Because of the very restricted airport facilities on the Island, the air service at the present time is, of necessity, operated by obsolete aircraft, but the airport is about to be upgraded and specially modified jets introduced. There is also a fairly regular shipping connection from both Sydney and Auckland.

There is a fast and efficient cable link between Sydney and the Island but, at the present time, no telephone link. However, a modern radio telephone system is at present being installed and should be operative by early 1972.

Government

Norfolk Island was annexed to the British Government by Captain Cook in 1774 and has remained a British Crown Colony ever since, although for practical purposes it is administered from Australia. The present control exercised by Australia is authorized by Orders in Council issued by the British Government in 1914.

The Australian Department of External Territories in Canberra appoints an Administrator who is legally responsible for the government of the island. He is the Chairman of the Norfolk Island Council, which consists of 8 members elected by the people on a democratic basis, with the Administrator as an ex-officio member. Although from a constitutional point of view its powers are only advisory, it is steadily growing in status and it is clear that, particularly with the rapidly increasing sophistication of life in Norfolk Island, the wishes of the people for the island concerning their own government, as expressed through the Council, will of necessity have to be paid more heed to in Canberra, where the actual Ordinances, under which the Island is governed, are promulgated.

Law

The law in force in Norfolk Island is based on British common law, as varied by certain laws of the State of New South Wales which have been made to apply to the Island and by specified Ordinances promulgated by the Australian Government to apply to the Island. The Trustee Act of New South Wales applies to the Island and the present company legislation is based on the English Companies Act of 1866, although it has been recently modernized, but the fairly extensive alterations do not prevent the speedy and relatively inexpensive incorporation of companies. Generally speaking, the present company law is well suited to a tax haven, although the Administration now makes a fairly substantial annual charge for maintaining a company on the Island. This is, however, in line with other similar centres elsewhere.

Language

The language of the Island is English.

Currency and Exchange Control

The currency of Norfolk Island is the Australian dollar, which is rapidly becoming recognized throughout the world as one of the stronger currencies. Australia (and hence Norfolk Island) is a member of the sterling area, but a large part of Australia's very substantial overseas reserves are held outside the sterling area. The Australian dollar has just been revalued against the American dollar and at the present time the former is worth approximately 119 cents U.S. There are no currency restrictions between Australia and Norfolk Island.

Because Norfolk Island uses Australian currency, it is subject to the same exchange control regulations as Australia itself. These regulations are administered by the Reserve Bank of Australia and whilst technically stringent, as a matter of firm policy of the Australian Government, they are administered in a very liberal manner with the deliberate view of attracting overseas investment into Australia.

Whilst the Reserve Bank of Australia cannot give an unconditional guarantee that capital moneys brought into Australia (and hence into Norfolk Island) can be repatriated at any time in the future, the Bank is prepared to indicate that, given a continuation of normal economic conditions, such approval would be granted. For practical purposes there are no difficulties associated with the remission of dividends or interest overseas.

There are no difficulties in the way of incorporating companies in Norfolk Island for foreign residents and indeed this is quite common.

Once the overseas funds have been subscribed to the Norfolk Island company, there is no restriction on how these funds may be invested in Australia. If the funds of the Norfolk Island company are to be invested outside Australia, Reserve Bank of Australia approval should be sought. This would normally be forthcoming if the funds emanate from external area sources.

Financial and Professional Services

The unique tax laws of Norfolk Island are only now being fully recognized and it is expected that this recognition will widen considerably in the near future. However, there already exist the necessary essential facilities for a fully comprehensive service to overseas investors. Both the Commonwealth Trading Bank of Australia, which is owned by the Australian Government, and the Bank of New South Wales, which is the oldest and largest publicly owned bank in Australia, have modern fully equipped branches on the island and are geared to cope with international transactions at all levels. A leading publicly incorporated trustee company is fully equipped to offer a wide range of services including, apart from acting as trustee for family trusts, the provision of directors, managers and secretaries for privately owned corporations and the ancillary service to make such companies fully operational. There are a number of competent lawyers and accountants, most with strong affiliations with major Australian firms. Generally speaking, their fees are based on current Australian fees with a small loading to cover increased overheads. Accordingly, the cost of setting up and maintaining an operation in Norfolk Island is considerably less than in other equivalent venues offering similar advantages. There are also a number of private individuals of impeccable integrity and considerable experience who provide management services.

At the present time there is no stock exchange on Norfolk Island but the establishment of such a body in the reasonably near future is a distinct possibility.

Internal Tax Structure

Apart from a very small tax on certain imports, which is marginal, there are no taxes of any kind whatsoever on Norfolk Island, in respect of income earned on the Island. For practical purposes, companies incorporated in Norfolk Island on behalf of non-residents of Australia are in the same position as ordinary residents of Norfolk Island. Such residents are, as the law stands at the present time, technically liable to pay Australian income tax on income derived from sources in Australia or overseas. However, there are numerous relatively simple and inexpensive ways whereby income can be derived in Norfolk Island even though the assets, from which some or all of the income may emanate, may be invested in Australia or elsewhere. There are at present two appeals pending before the full High Court of Australia which may decide, *inter alia*, whether the present Australian taxing laws relating to the Australian income of Norfolk Island residents are valid under the terms of the Australian Constitution and, if the present law is found to be invalid, the scope of Norfolk Island as a tax haven will be increased even further, at least in the short run.

The general exemption from taxation referred to at the beginning of this chapter extends to freedom from death duty and stamp duty, which is of very great importance in the field of planning family estates.

There is some uncertainty at the present time as to the liability to Australian withholding tax of dividends and interest paid by Norfolk Island resident companies to persons or corporations overseas. Where such payments are contemplated, professional advice should be obtained in each specific case.

Tax Treaties

The Island enjoys the benefit of double taxation agreements made between Australia and other countries.

Available Entities

The same means of carrying on business are available in Norfolk Island as elsewhere in countries whose laws are based on those of the United Kingdom. For instance, people can trade under their own name or in partnership, but the taxation benefits of doing so, as far as non-residents of Norfolk Island are concerned, are minimal, unless the person concerned also lives in another tax haven.

The Company

Companies incorporated overseas can be registered in Norfolk Island as foreign companies and can do in Norfolk Island everything which the company can do pursuant to its original Charter or other constituting document. In order to obtain registration as a foreign company in Norfolk Island, it is necessary to lodge with the Registrar of Companies a copy of the memorandum and articles of association or other document covering the constitution of the corporation, duly certified by the appropriate government official responsible for the administering of the corporation in the place of incorporation. It is also necessary to file a copy, similarly certified, of the company's certificate of incorporation or other similar evidence that the corporation exists as such. Where these documents are in a language other than English, it is necessary for them to be translated into English, with the translations being duly certified as correct. It is also necessary for the foreign corporation to appoint, under seal, a person resident in Norfolk Island to act as the agent of the company.

It is desirable that corporations seeking to register in Norfolk Island as foreign companies obtain local legal advice on the exact requirements.

In almost all cases, the most appropriate avenue for utilizing the advantages of Norfolk Island is the incorporation of a company or companies.

The law relating to the incorporation and management of companies in Norfolk Island is contained in the Companies Ordinance 1926–1971, which is an amalgum of the English Companies Act of 1866 with substantial additions based on contemporary Australian company law. The newly amended Ordinance whilst generally upgrading the law, is still appropriate to the needs of a modern tax haven.

Generally, incorporation is handled by a lawyer either resident on Norfolk Island or who has knowledge of the local laws. It is necessary to prepare a memorandum and articles of association in each case in the form most appropriate to the needs of the proposed company and the persons on whose behalf it is being established. At the present time, there must be a minimum of seven shareholders, and, although these need not necessarily be Norfolk Islanders, it is most convenient, in normal cases, to use residents for this purpose.

The memorandum of association must contain the following information:

(*a*) the name of the company;
(*b*) the location of the registered office;
(*c*) the objects for which the company is being established;
(*d*) a declaration that the liability of the members of the company is limited;
(*e*) the nominal share capital of the company.

The articles of association provide for the control of the company and regulate the rights of the shareholders amongst themselves. In most cases, these are fairly standard. It is normal to provide that meetings of directors and/or shareholders can be held anywhere in the world and, although there is no restriction on appointing foreign directors, it is usual, as a matter of convenience, to appoint local directors.

As mentioned earlier, there are a number of people on the Island with suitable experience and integrity to operate companies, and where the companies are not themselves offering their shares to members of the general public, but are of a private nature, the local trustee company is prepared to act in this regard.

It is possible for a Norfolk Island company to issue debentures, either secured or unsecured, and also to issue bearer shares. The amended Companies Ordinance now makes provision for the issue of redeemable preference shares, which is a useful adjunct to tax planning arrangements.

Norfolk Island companies are required to keep at their registered offices registers of directors and members, together with minute books and a register of charges which may have been given over the assets of the company. Annual returns must be filed with the Registrar of Companies on the Island, setting out shareholders, directors and other officers, the registered office, the issued share capital and a balance sheet which in some cases requires to be audited. It is essential that each company keep the Registrar informed of its registered office for the time being, and this must be displayed prominently in the place where the office is established.

The cost of incorporating a company in Norfolk Island, including all necessary disbursements and the directors' fees, secretarial expenses and registered office fees for the first year, is usually in the vicinity of $850 and thereafter the annual cost of administering the company in a normal case, including the provision of directors, a registered office and the preparation and filing of all necessary returns, would not exceed $500 Australian. However, after the first year of a company's operation, it is necessary to pay an annual filing fee to the Administration of $250 Australian. This amount, although substantial, is in line with fees being introduced in other similar havens.

Where the company has a large capital or a complicated memorandum and articles of association, the initial cost will be somewhat higher and where the company transacts a large amount of business, the annual operating cost will also be relatively higher.

One special advantage arising from the use of companies in relation to tax planning in Norfolk Island is the fact that they are not required to pass on profits earned by way of dividends. Instead, the profits can be capitalized and re-invested, thus rendering it possible to compound the tax savings involved.

The Trust

Norfolk Island trusts are in most respects similar to trusts which can be created under English Law although there are certain differences. A modern Trustee Companies Ordinance is about to be promulgated, which will further enhance the status of the Island. The Norfolk Island trustee company can be appointed as sole trustee and given wide powers as to both investment of the funds from time to time and also, by way of discretionary trusts, with regard to the ultimate distribution of the funds of the trust amongst a given class of beneficiaries. It is usually desirable, and in some cases essential, for the trust to be set up in conjunction with the establishment of one or more companies.

PANAMA

INTERNATIONAL SERVICE COMPANY INC.

The Republic of Panama lies between North and South America and it has an area of approximately 29,700 square miles, including the Canal Zone. Panama has an estimated population of 1,450,000, about 60 per cent rural and 40 per cent urban. Panama is the largest city with about 500,000 inhabitants. Colon is the main port on the Atlantic side; its population is about 100,000. Climate is tropical with heavy rains. Annual rainfall is about 70 inches on the Pacific side and about 150 inches on the Atlantic side. The dry season lasts from mid-December through end of April; the rest of the year is rainy.

Communications

Excellent transport facilities are available by air, sea or through the Inter-American Highway. Tocumen International Airport, located about 15 miles from the city of Panama is served by 14 foreign and 4 Panamanian airlines. Cristobal and Balboa at the two ends of the Panama Canal, Puerto Armuelles in the Province of Chiriqui and the "Bahia de las Minas" have modern port facilities for ocean-going ships. Highway transportation is good through the Inter-American Highway, the Trans-Isthmian Highway and the many other highways and roads. It is possible to travel by road from Alaska to Panama City. Feasibility studies were completed and a highway through the Darien jungles is now under construction to connect the northern with the southern continent.

Panama's telephone, telegraph and mail services are the best in Latin America. During September 1968 international telephone communication system through satellite was installed.

Government

Panama has a centralized republican form of government. The President, as Chief Executive of the Republic, is elected by direct popular vote for four years; the President cannot be re-elected immediately following a term of office. Deputies of the National Assembly—42 in total—which is Panama's unicameral parliament, are also elected by popular vote for a period of four years concurrently with the term of the President. Deputies can be re-elected. Presently a provisional Government is in power headed by a civilian President and a civilian member of the Junta.

Language

The official language of Panama is Spanish, but English is widely used. This is so perhaps because English is used almost exclusively in the Canal Zone. Most of the businessmen and professionals as well as clerks and stenographers in the two principal cities (Panama and Colon) are bilingual. There are three English language newspapers in the Republic of Panama.

Currency and Exchange Control

Panama's Balboa is at par and freely exchangeable with the U.S. dollar. Panama has no paper currency and the U.S. currency and coins together with Panamanian coins are the medium of exchange.

Panama does not have a central bank and has no exchange control. There is no tax on transfer of funds of any nature. Bank accounts are payable in both Panamanian Balboas and in U.S. dollars. Panama has no restrictions whatsoever on the in and out movement of funds.

Panama banks have numbered accounts, the laws governing numbered accounts are about the same as those governing Swiss numbered bank accounts.

Financial and Professional Services

Panama has excellent locally and internationally trained lawyers. Incorporation of Panama companies as well as any other legal service can be obtained through the many competent attorneys swiftly and without red tape.

Most of the large international auditing firms are locally established

(Price Waterhouse & Co.; Peat, Marwick, Mitchell & Co.; Librent, Ross & Montgomery; Haskins & Sells; Ernst & Ernst; Touche, Ross & Co.; Arthur Andersen & Co.; Arthur Young & Co.; Main Lafretz & Co., *etc.*). Accountants and auditors are in abundance.

Several stock brokerage firms are established in Panama. Merrill Lynch, Pierce, Fenner & Smith has its Latin American Office in Panama. Local offices of international fund sales organizations are established as well.

Per capita, Panama has the largest banking facilities in Latin America. There are at the present 26 locally and foreign owned banking institutions in Panama. Banco Nacional is the largest local chain of banks; this is a semi-autonomous institute of the Panama Government. More notable private banks are: The First National City Bank of New York, the Chase Manhatten Bank, Bank of America, First National Bank of Chicago, Marine Midland Bank, Panama Bank & Trust Co. (affiliate of Banque Nationale de Paris, France), Bank of London & Montreal, Ltd., Algemene Nederland Bank, Swiss Bank Corporation (Overseas) Ltd., Banco General, Banco Mercantil Panameño, International Bank and Finance Corporation, Banco Interoceanico de Comercio, Banco Alemán-Panameño. Colombian Banks: Banco de Colombia, Banco de Bogotá, Banco Cafetero, Banco del Comercio. Spanish Banks: Banco Exterior, Banco de Santander.

A number of management companies offer specialized services to foreign base corporations, including trust, consulting, administrative, accounting and clerical services. The services of these firms range from co-ordination of the activities involved in the incorporation of a Panama company to the provision for their clients' companies of directors and officers or of complete management services.

Internal Tax Structure

Panama's income tax law is based on the principles of territoriality. Consequently income tax is levied only upon net income derived from operations within the territorial boundaries of the Republic of Panama. These basic principles have been maintained, without change, since the foundation of the Republic in 1903.

The new income tax law of Panama (Law No. 9 of 23rd December, 1964—Chapter 1, Article 694, Proviso 2), clearly defines the activities which are not subject to Panama income tax:

(*a*) Invoicing, from an office established in Panama, the sale of merchandise or products for a sum higher than at which said products or merchandise had been invoiced to the office established in Panama, provided that said merchandise or products are handled exclusively abroad.

(*b*) Directing, from an office established in Panama, operations which are completed, consummated or take effect abroad; and

(*c*) Distributing dividends or participations from juridical persons when said dividends or participations are derived from income not produced within the territory of the Republic of Panama, including the income derived from activities mentioned in subdivision (*a*) and (*b*) of this Proviso.

On the basis of the above clearly defined provisions of the Panama Income Tax Law, Panamanian corporations or local branches of foreign corporations with established offices and employees in Panama do not pay Panamanian income tax on their net profits if such offices merely direct the purchases and sales but the merchandise never physically comes through Panama.

Royalties, interest, dividends, commissions, profits on trading and other income received from foreign sources are not subject to Panama income taxes. Panama corporations may pay out such income as dividends (or in any other form) to its shareholders, free of Panama income tax. Interest on time deposits placed with local banks is not subject to Panama income tax.

Foreign citizens who are resident in Panama and physically located within the Republic of Panama must pay Panama income tax on their remuneration. The income tax on individuals ranges from 2 per cent for the first $1,000 income to 46 per cent over $200,000. If an employee (or resident director) travels away from Panama for more than 180 days during any given year, his salary can be pro-rated between the time he was physically present in Panama and the time he was absent from the country and he will pay tax on his proportionate income when he was present here.

There is no inheritance tax on securities of a Panama company whose assets are largely invested outside of Panama. Panamanian laws are very liberal concerning inheritance tax liabilities. Such taxes depend on the degree of relationship and on the amount of inheritance. Only estates appraised at more than U.S.$30,000 are taxed.

The tax ranges from 4 per cent for closest relatives on $5,000 to

33·75 per cent for non-relatives over $400,000. It is assessed on tangible assets located in Panama or on securities issued by Panama companies whose capital is largely invested in Panama. The important advantage of Panama's inheritance tax law is that the estate is divided first among the beneficiaries before the tax is determined. This provision is indeed important because the tax is based on rising scale in direct proportion to the amount of inheritance. Another important provision of the law is that an allowance is given to each beneficiary for a 20 per cent deduction of the tax liability.

Panama Laws do not provide for immunity from taxes. However, no such immunity is necessary for a person resident outside of Panama since his non-Panamanian earnings, as indicated elsewhere in this chapter, are not subject to Panama income tax.

If wilful evasion of taxes (of any kind) or fraud is proven in courts by Panama Government tax authorities, penalties are imposed to the extent of from two to ten times the amount of taxes.

Other Considerations

Ship registration under the Panama Flag is widely used by international shipping companies. This is due primarily to the very low registration taxes as compared to other countries throughout the world. Registration tax is $1 per net ton; Government fee for registration of bill of sale is 20¢ per net ton; these two taxes are payable once only. Annual tax is 10¢ per net ton. Liberal labour laws concerning Panama flag vessels are also an important consideration. Income earned on international shipping activities are specifically and expressly exempted from Panama income taxes.

Tax Treaties

The Republic of Panama does not have tax treaties with any country.

Available Entities

The following commercial entities exist under the Panamanian Commercial Code: corporation; general partnership; limited partnership; stock issuing limited partnership; co-operative company and single proprietorship. Most business enterprises however are conducted in the Republic of Panama in the form of corporations, partnerships or proprietorship. Almost without exception, foreign base operations are conducted through corporations.

The Company

Panamanian corporations may be organized by two persons of legal age (who can be Panamanian or foreigners) for any lawful purpose (or purposes) whereby the incorporators subscribe to at least one share each to the stock of the corporation under formation. In practice, two persons from the incorporating attorneys' office act as incorporators and immediately upon incorporation the two persons endorse (in blank) their subscription rights. The authorized capital stock of a Panama corporation does not have to be fully subscribed or paid up. The incorporating attorney or firm of attorneys may subsequently act as the statutory resident agent of the corporation.

The following details are required to incorporate a Panama company:

(1) The name of the corporation. The name must include any of the following words or abbreviations: Corporations, Corp., Incorporated, Inc., Sociedad Anónima, S.A.

(2) The specified objects of the corporation. Usually broad general objects are listed for corporations; however, specific mention is made in the corporate charter of the main objects for which the corporation is organized.

(3) The amount of authorized capital, stating also the number of shares and their respective par values, if any. (If no par value capital is registered, then the Panama government values each share at $20 for purposes of computation of registration tax on authorized capital).

(4) The type of shares—nominative or bearer, common or preferred, and the class of shares—class A or class B, voting or non-voting.

(5) The full names and addresses of at least three directors (no abbreviations are accepted). If so desired, the services of directors and officers are provided for a yearly fee by local management companies.

(6) The full names and addresses of the first officers: president, secretary and treasurer. (One person may hold two positions, but the president cannot be the secretary as well. Directors may

also act as officers. Directors and officers do not have to be shareholders.) Although the corporation law does not require listing of officers in the original corporate charter, the first officers are usually used so as to avoid the expense and loss of time in preparing new minutes and registering them in the Public Registry.

(7) Duration of the corporation.
(8) Name and address of the Resident Agent.
(9) Domicile of the company.

A Capital Stock Tax is payable once only, upon registration of the corporate charter in the Panamanian Public Registry (Mercantile Section):

\$20 (minimum Tax) on the first	\$10,000
\$0·75 per \$1,000 on next	\$90,000
\$0·50 per \$1,000 on next	\$900,000
\$0·10 per \$1,000 on excess over	\$1,000,000

The formation of a Panama company takes from 10 days to two weeks. It costs about \$300, plus expenses. The expenses depend on the amount of the authorized capital stock. Other expenses include notarial fees which might amount to about \$100 depending on the length of the corporate charter document. If a Panama company does not operate locally (having an office in Panama through which the direction of international operations is performed does not constitute "doing business in Panama" under Panamanian income tax law), such company can maintain its books of accounts in any manner it desires and anywhere in the world. The law requires, however, that a Panama company must have a minute book and a stock register book; these are bound books and they are rubricated by a judge from the local courts. Other locally operating companies must maintain, in addition to the above, the following bound and rubricated books: general ledger, general journal and inventory and balance sheet book. Any company not physically engaged in business locally (although it might have an office in Panama to direct international business activities) does not have to have commercial licence.

Under its corporation law, the Republic of Panama allows people of any nationality to act as directors or officers of Panama corporations. Such directors or officers do not have to be residents of Panama. There are no restrictions imposed by law or local regulations which would not permit Panama companies to do business with any particular country. Every Panama company must have a resident agent. Such an agent must be an attorney. Traditionally a yearly fee of from $100 to $200 is charged for a resident agency. The resident agent does not have to file any reports to the Panama Government; he is the liaison between the corporation and the Panama Government.

It follows that a Panama corporation, whatever its capital, suffers no Panama income tax on its net profit if the income is earned from foreign sources or consists of interest on local time deposits.

Incorporating cost of a corporation with $10,000 capital might be about the following:

Notorial expenses including Government stamped paper	$100
Capital Stock Tax on $10,000	20
Public Registry fees and expenses	20
Legal fees	300
Minute Book and Stock Register Book	20
Rubrication of above two Books	10
Miscellaneous other charges	10
Total	$480

Canal Zone

The Canal Zone is a strip of land across the country connecting the Pacific with the Atlantic Ocean. The Canal Zone, use of which was granted in perpetuity to the United States under a Treaty which is now being renegotiated, is about 50 miles long and 10 miles wide. Its population is about 40,000. There are no commercial establishments in the Canal Zone and residents in the area obtain most of their supplies from commissaries; restaurants, clubs, theatres, *etc.* are restricted to residents in the Canal Zone, members or employees of the Armed Forces or to other employees of the Panama Canal Company. Only those employed in the Canal Zone and their dependents are permitted to reside there.

Colon Free Zone

The Colon Free Zone, located at the Atlantic entrance to the Panama Canal, is the focal point for sea and air transportation in the hemisphere. It is considered a unique entrepôt of world commerce. The annual volume of business is approximately $400 million and there are as many as 400 international companies established in the Zone from U.S., European, Japanese and other origins. Merchandise is received in bulk duty free, subsequently being repacked, labelled, assembled, manufactured (as the case may be) and reshipped in smaller quantities to customers in a wide area. Companies operating in the Colon Free Zone do not require a commercial licence.

Operations in the Colon Free Zone may be conducted through any of the following methods:

(1) The user may lease land from the Colon Free Zone at 15¢ per square metre per month and construct its own building. The Land lease can be signed for 20 years with options for renewal.
(2) The user may lease warehouse space owned by the Colon Free Zone. Rental is from 75¢ down to 63¢ per square metre per month depending on size of the building and on lease period.
(3) Public warehouse. When volume of business does not warrant the customer to set up its own warehouse operations in the Colon Free Zone, a service company can provide all the services in behalf of the customer. Charges are made monthly based on merchandise warehoused.

Companies established in the Colon Free Zone might have three types of income subject to different income tax consequences:

(1) Income derived from triangular indent sales when merchandise does not physically come to the Colon Free Zone (the merchandise is sold through the Colon Free Zone company but physically the merchandise moves from the seller to the buyer direct and only the shipping documents are handled by the Free Zone company). In this instance the profit is not subject to Panama income taxes.
(2) Net income derived through re-exporting of the merchandise to foreign countries, is subject to Panama income taxes (on the basis of the 1954 income tax law—which is substantially lower than the 1964 tax rates) minus 90 per cent discount.
(3) Net income derived on sales to the Republic of Panama is subject to full current Panama income tax.

SWITZERLAND

FLURI + GREUTERT, TRUST AND AUDITING COMPANY LIMITED.

Switzerland has developed into an important international economic and finance centre in Europe. This progress is due to its liberal economical policy, its solid political situation, the stability of its currency, the pleasant living conditions and its relatively favourable tax legislation.

Are the tax rates higher in Switzerland than elsewhere? This question has been examined for the five big Common Market countries, England, Sweden and the two important overseas industrial countries, United States and Japan (*Economie et Statistique*, pamphlet April 1970; *Statistische Werke der Schweiz*, 1. XII. 1969). In the comparative table below the result is shown between the total tax payments and the gross national product:

Country	*Total tax burden*	*Average increase from 1959 to 1967*
Sweden	33·7	3·1
Western Germany	24·8	0·8
Great Britain	28·0	1·6
Netherlands	24·5	1·4
U.S.A.	23·1	0·2
Belgium	22·8	2·2
France	22·5	0·2
Italy	20·1	1·0
Japan	15·3	1·0
Switzerland	16·4	—

The difference is made even more obvious by adding the compulsory social contributions to the tax burdens:

Sweden	40·8	4·5
Western Germany	35·1	0·8
Great Britain	32·8	2·0
Netherlands	37·2	3·0

U.S.A.	28·3	1·0
Belgium	32·6	3·4
France	36·6	1·0
Italy	30·8	1·7
Japan	19·0	0·8
Switzerland	25·0	—

Switzerland is a member of various important international organizations, *i.e.* E.F.T.A., G.A.T.T., O.E.C.D., U.N.C.T.A.D. Although Switzerland is not a member of the U.N.O. it works together with this organization and the World Bank in many fields. Since the formation of the Common Market and E.F.T.A. many foreign companies have established subsidiaries or holding companies in Switzerland, so being able better to take care of their interests in Europe.

Communications

Situated in the centre of Europe, at the meeting point of the most important main roads from north to south and west to east, Switzerland offers business circles interested in export excellent site conditions. By means of a highly developed road and railway system all markets can be reached quickly and punctually, and the waterway navigable from the open sea to Basle makes up for the disadvantage of Switzerland being a landlocked country. An intensive international air traffic connects the main Swiss airports Zurich-Kloten, Basle and Geneva-Cointrin with the most important European and American cities as well as with Asia and Africa. The telephone and telex system with the most modern equipment, a considerable transportation system, an insurance system of international reputation as well as a financially solid banking system with world wide connections, support and facilitate the export business. Its beautiful countryside and its first class tourist facilities make Switzerland, although also an industrial country, very attractive for visitors.

Government

The fundamental law of the Swiss Confederation is the Constitution, accepted in 1848 and revised in 1874. In 123 articles the rights and duties of the citizen and the federal authorities are laid down. Switzerland is a federal republic divided into 25 cantons which exercise all rights not transferred to the Federal Government. The two dominant principles of the Swiss Constitution are federalism and democracy. The power of government of the Swiss Confederation is executed by the *Bundesrat*, consisting of seven members. The internal political situation is peaceful and solid. As to foreign policy the guiding principle of Switzerland for centuries is neutrality.

Law

The basis of the Swiss law is the civil law.

Language

German, French, Italian and Rhaeto-Romanic (which originates from Latin) are the official languages in Switzerland. Most of the population in Switzerland speaks the German language in various dialects. Since English as well as French is taught in high schools, a lot of Swiss, especially businessmen, are fully conversant with English.

Currency and Exchange Control

The currency is the Swiss franc which, due to its stability, has contributed a great deal to a prosperity which can hardly be found in any other European country. There do not exist any exchange restrictions in Switzerland.

Financial and Professional Services

The Swiss banking system maintains its own foreign agencies and correspondents all over the world. The bank secret is strictly kept. There are no problems in finding excellent trained and experienced lawyers, accountants, stockbrokers and investment advisers.

Internal Tax Structure

The Swiss tax system follows the structure of the Federal Government. Besides the federal tax law there exist separate tax laws for the 25 different cantons. A company with a capital has to pay a tax on its net profit as well as an additional tax on its capital to the Federal Government and to all cantons. Contrary to foreign countries the tax on net profit of companies is progressive. The progression depends on the intensity of profit, *i.e.* the relation between profit and invested capital. A high yield leads to a high tax rate, a small yield to a low tax rate. For example, a net profit equivalent to a yield of 10 per cent, gives rise to a tax rate of 5 per cent, while for the same net profit, equivalent to a yield of 6 per cent, the tax rate is only 3 per cent. The maximum fiscal charges by the cantons and communities will amount to approximately 25 to 35 per cent. Other countries usually have a proportional tax system on the net profits of companies and the rates are comparatively high, amounting to approximately 50 per cent of the net profit.

As in comparable industrial countries, private individuals in Switzerland are affected by income tax imposed on personal income, *i.e.* income from work, property and rights as well as shares in net profits of private enterprises and profit originating from participations in companies with a capital. The progression of the income tax is adjusted to the amount of the total income. This means that the effective tax rate for income originating from private enterprises and income on shares in companies depends on the amount of the net income.

Holding companies are granted tax advantages by the Government and nearly all cantons. The Federal Government grants a reduction on income tax (amounting to between 2·85 and 7·60 per cent for companies with commercial activities) to companies with interests of at least 20 per cent, or of two million francs, in the stock capital of other internal or external companies in the proportion to which the income on such participations (holding income) bears to the entire gross profit. This reduction is also granted if the interests in other companies do not represent the main purpose and main activity of the company. In this respect, only those amounts are accepted as holding income which are paid in respect of the shares held by the holding company, *e.g.* dividends, profits on liquidations; interest on advances and fees from licences granted to the affiliated companies do not qualify as holding income. If the entire gross profit originates from holding income, the company will have to pay no tax on net profit but only tax on capital, the rate of which amounts to 0·75 per cent on share capital and reserves. Holding companies are also privileged by the cantons; generally, they have to pay only a small tax on capital and no tax on net profit.

Furthermore, many cantonal tax laws grant the same or similar tax privileges as are granted to the holding companies to the so-called domiciliary companies. Basically, this domiciliary privilege means that no tax has to be paid on profits and only a reduced tax on capital will be charged. A company is considered a domiciliary company when—not being a holding company—it is legally domiciled in the canton but neither owns real estate there nor handles its affairs there by its own staff. In this category belong, for example, patent companies, the income of which originates from external licence fees, as also do companies owning real estate in foreign countries or realizing profits out of transactions which are concluded and carried through abroad, *i.e.* not affecting Switzerland. The income of all these companies comes from abroad. Where a company maintains its own offices and its own staff, it will in some cantons not be privileged as a domiciliary company. Therefore, domiciliary companies generally maintain their legal domicile with a trust company or a lawyer, where the administration will be executed according to the instructions of the client.

Some cantons also grant tax privileges to so-called "mixed" companies. These are companies which besides participation and domicile functions also have certain business activities.

A mixed company pays its taxes at the full rates on capital invested in and earnings derived from Swiss real estate and, in general, on all income arising from Swiss sources, but may still be treated as a holding or domiciliary company as regards its other assets and income.

Newly established companies may be especially privileged, according to the actual circumstances, in some cantons.

Base and domiciliary companies generally are founded in the form of a joint stock company, the capital of which, being determined in advance, is divided into shares. Shareholders can be domestic or foreign private individuals or companies. The death of a shareholder does not lead to a liquidation of the company and creates no special tax problems.

Stamp Duties

Stamp duties in Switzerland are of minor importance. Upon the formation of a Swiss joint stock company a once-and-for-all federal stamp duty of 2 per cent on the capital must be paid, which is based on the nominal value of the issued share capital. A premium, therefore, may be considered. If shares are not wholly paid up, stamp duty of 1 per cent on the uncalled capital will have to be paid. The rest of the 1 per cent is due when the remaining amount is paid up. The cantons do not charge any taxes for incorporation.

Turnover Tax

On the internal delivery of goods by a wholesale dealer against payment, a turnover tax is charged. No turnover tax is paid if internal deliveries are destined for immediate export by the purchaser, nor is it paid on goods in transit. The imported goods are taxable and a tax rate of 4 to 6 per cent (on the value of the goods) is payable. Furthermore, import duties will be charged at specific rates by weight, which vary according to the description of goods.

Withholding Tax

The withholding tax is the only Swiss federal tax levied at source; it is applicable to dividends of Swiss companies (including the distribution of profits on liquidation) as well as to the interest from bonds and bank deposits. Its rate amounts to 30 per cent. Shareholders and Loan creditors living in Switzerland may claim a refund of tax, as opposed to residents of foreign countries who can only claim a refund of tax if it is provided for in a treaty for the avoidance of double taxation. There exist numerous tax treaties with other countries which provide for reductions of withholding taxes up to at least 50 per cent. The agreement with Great Britain, Ireland and the Netherlands provide a special reduction (down to 5 or 0 per cent) for holdings with an interest of at least 25 per cent in the distributing Swiss company.

For licence fees, paid by domiciliary companies, private individuals or corporations, no withholding taxes are paid. Therefore, a Swiss joint stock company can pay licence fees without any tax reduction to patent or licence owners domiciled in Switzerland or abroad.

Tax Treaties

Contrary to many other states which are known as tax havens, Switzerland has the great advantage of having tax treaties for the avoidance of double taxation with the following countries:

Western Germany	Great Britain	Sweden
Denmark	Ireland	Spain
Austria	The Netherlands	U.S.A.
Finland	Norway	South Africa
France	Pakistan	

The following table shows the tax reliefs granted to Swiss companies on dividends and interest:

	External tax rate	*Relief*	*Remaining Taxes*
Western Germany			
dividends	25·75	10·75	15[1]
interest from conversion loans and bonds	25·75	10·75	15
interest from fixed-yield securities	25·75	25·75	—
Denmark			
dividends	30	30	—
Austria			
dividends	19·6	19·6	—
Finland			
dividends	15	10	5[2]
France			
dividends	25	10	15
interest	25	15	10
Great Britain			
dividends	38·75	23·75	15[3]
interest	38·75	38·75	—
Ireland			
interest	35	35	—

	External tax rate	Relief	Remaining Taxes
Netherlands			
dividends	25	10	15[4]
Norway			
dividends	25	20	5
Pakistan			
dividends	15/20	5/10	10[5]
Sweden			
dividends	30	25	5
Spain			
dividends	15	5	10[6]
interest	24	14	10[7]
U.S.A.			
dividends	30	15	15[8]
interest	30	25	5
South Africa			
dividends	15	7·5	7·5

Notes

(1) Swiss companies with holdings of at least 25 per cent have no claim for refund.
(2) For corporations.
(3) The rate is reduced to 5 per cent for minimum holdings of 25 per cent.
(4) For minimum holdings of 25 per cent, full relief.
(5) Only for holdings of at least $33\frac{1}{3}$ per cent, and in industrial concerns.
(6) Only for minimum holdings of 25 per cent.
(7) For interest on long-term bank loans: full relief.
(8) With minimum holdings of 95 per cent: only 5 per cent.

The advantages of the double taxation agreements are only granted to persons who, according to the treaties, are allowed to claim for it. A claim for tax relief by a private individual, a company or a partnership resident or domiciled in Switzerland, which might lead to direct or indirect tax relief of non-privileged persons, is considered an improper claim. To prevent the abuse of double tax agreements Swiss companies in which non-Swiss have a considerable interest can only claim relief from foreign taxes if they conform to the following conditions:

not more than 50 per cent of the income for which tax relief is claimed may be used to satisfy the rights or claims of persons not resident or domiciled in Switzerland, for example, for payment of credits and licence fees of aliens, the credit may not exceed 6 per cent;

the credits may not exceed six times the amount of capital and declared reserves;

corporations and co-operative societies must, during each annual accounting period, distribute at least 25 per cent of the gross income to which a tax convention applies.

Available Entities

In Switzerland the following entities are recognized by law:

general partnership;
unlimited and limited partnership;
joint stock company;
partnership limited by shares;
private limited liability company;
co-operative society;
foundation.

Of these entities, the joint stock company and the private limited liability company are most used, and these are discussed below.

The Joint Stock Company

The joint stock company is, due to its flexibility and very little publicity, the most suitable and most used legal form of base company. To establish a joint stock company at least three shareholders are necessary who might be private individuals or corporations. Where there is only one shareholder, the two additional shareholders can be represented by trustees.

The articles of incorporation of a joint stock company must include conditions with respect to the following points:

name of corporation;
purpose of corporation;
amount of share capital and nominal value of shares;
organization of the corporation and its representation;
calling of the general meeting of the shareholders and the right to vote.

The nominal share capital must amount to at least 50,000 francs divided into nominal shares of at least 100 francs each. Shares without nominal value are not permitted in Switzerland. The shares can be made out as bearer or registered shares. Bearer shares can only be issued upon full payment of the full nominal value. Registered shares have to be subscribed up to at least 20 per cent of the nominal value, and the total amount subscribed must not be less than 20,000 francs. The transfer of shares can be limited by the articles. The share capital of a corporation can also be covered by an investment in kind. Shares are commonly issued for cash, but they may also be issued in payment for the transfer to the company of an investment or other asset —for example the transfer of a right to participate in some enterprise —and in that case certain regulations for valuation must be observed. The incorporation of a joint stock company has to be done by a public deed and must be registered in the Commercial Register of the place of domicile. A notice of its registration is published in the official Swiss Trade Gazette, where the purpose, share capital and names of the members of the Board of Administrators are published, but not, however, the names of the founders. To establish a joint stock company is simple and can take place within a few days.

The governing bodies of the corporation are: the general meeting of the shareholders, the board of administrators and the auditors. The ultimate authority of the company derives from the general meeting of the shareholders. According to law the meeting of the shareholders is moreover competent to appoint the administrators and the auditors, to approve the annual business report and the annual balance sheet, to decide upon the use of net profits and to discharge the administration from liability for their actions as well as to amend the articles.

The board of administrators has all rights not passed on by law or the articles to another authority. With respect to the nationality of the administrators—though not to the nationality of the shareholders—there exist certain legal conditions. If only one administrator is appointed he must be a citizen of, and resident in, Switzerland. If the administration consists of more than one member, the majority of them must be citizens of, and resident in, Switzerland. Exceptions are only possible in holding companies, where the interests mainly consist of foreign business shares. The company is free to elect the management, *i.e.* managing directors and signing clerks. They may have any nationality or domicile and it is possible to have a "one-man" corporation.

Each member of the board of administrators must hold one share. The auditors, however, may neither belong to the board of administration nor be employees of the company. Private individuals or trust companies can be appointed auditors. The auditors have to examine the accounts and the annual balance sheet. The balance sheet is not required to be published.

The costs for the formation of a joint share company are the following:

(*a*) two per cent stamp duty for paid-up capital;
(*b*) registration fees of 2 per thousand of the paid-up capital, minimum 250 francs, maximum 6,000 francs;
(*c*) notarial fees and professional fees, approximately 1,500 francs to 2,000 francs (for companies with small capital).

The annual maintenance costs are dependent on the size of the activities of the company; for a small company with modest activity the annual costs will amount to 1,000 to 2,000 francs.

The Private Limited Liability Company

Entities established by persons resident or domiciled abroad are very often established in the form of a private limited liability company. This entity can be chosen not only for trading and manufacturing but also for other economic purposes. To establish a private limited liability company two promoters, either private individuals or companies, are necessary. There are no restrictions on the nationality of the owners. Administration and representation are fulfilled jointly by all owners unless they have not been passed on by law or articles to one or more owners or to a person not being an owner. At least one manager must be resident in, but not necessarily a citizen of, Switzerland. All owners of a private limited liability company must be registered in the Commercial Register; with a joint stock company only shares belonging to the board of administrators require registration and other shareholders preserve their anonymity. The ultimate authority of the private limited liability company derives from the company meeting.

The minimum capital must be not less than 20,000 francs, the maximum capital not more than a million francs. To establish a private limited liability company at least 50 per cent of the entire capital must be paid-up in cash or kind. The owners are liable as joint debtors, but only up to the amount of the registered capital.

The fulfilment of all requirements by law are sufficient for the formation and registration of a company. There do not exist any additional restrictions. However, it has to be observed that a company established according to civil law can be refused as tax subject by the fiscal authorities where such a company has only been established for the purpose of tax evasion or other tax manipulations.